# Knowledge assets
# Complete Self-Assessment Guide

C000060616

The guidance in this Self-Assessment is based
practices and standards in business process architecture, design and
quality management. The guidance is also based on the professional
judgment of the individual collaborators listed in the Acknowledgments.

## Notice of rights

## Trademarks

Copyright © by The Art of Service
http://theartofservice.com
service@theartofservice.com

# Table of Contents

# About The Art of Service

The Art of Service, Business Process Architects since 2000, is dedicated to helping stakeholders achieve excellence.

Defining, designing, creating, and implementing a process to solve a stakeholders challenge or meet an objective is the most valuable role… In EVERY group, company, organization and department.

Unless you're talking a one-time, single-use project, there should be a process. Whether that process is managed and implemented by humans, AI, or a combination of the two, it needs to be designed by someone with a complex enough perspective to ask the right questions.

Someone capable of asking the right questions and step back and say, 'What are we really trying to accomplish here? And is there a different way to look at it?'

With The Art of Service's Standard Requirements Self-Assessments, we empower people who can do just that — whether their title is marketer, entrepreneur, manager, salesperson, consultant, Business Process Manager, executive assistant, IT Manager, CIO etc... —they are the people who rule the future. They are people who watch the process as it happens, and ask the right questions to make the process work better.

**Contact us when you need any support with this Self-Assessment and any help with templates, blue-prints and examples of standard documents you might need:**

http://theartofservice.com
service@theartofservice.com

# Acknowledgments

This checklist was developed under the auspices of The Art of Service, chaired by Gerardus Blokdyk.

Representatives from several client companies participated in the preparation of this Self-Assessment.

In addition, we are thankful for the design and printing services provided.

# Included Resources - how to access

Included with your purchase of the book is the Knowledge assets Self-Assessment Spreadsheet Dashboard which contains all questions and Self-Assessment areas and auto-generates insights, graphs, and project RACI planning - all with examples to get you started right away.

How? Simply send an email to
**access@theartofservice.com**
with this books' title in the subject to get the Knowledge assets Self Assessment Tool right away.

You will receive the following contents with New and Updated specific criteria:

- The latest quick edition of the book in PDF

- The latest complete edition of the book in PDF, which criteria correspond to the criteria in...

- The Self-Assessment Excel Dashboard, and...

- Example pre-filled Self-Assessment Excel Dashboard to get familiar with results generation

- In-depth specific Checklists covering the topic

- Project management checklists and templates to assist with implementation

**INCLUDES LIFETIME SELF ASSESSMENT UPDATES**

Every self assessment comes with Lifetime Updates and Lifetime Free Updated Books. Lifetime Updates is an industry-first feature which allows you to receive verified self assessment updates, ensuring you always have the most accurate information at your fingertips.

Get it now- you will be glad you did - do it now, before you forget.

Send an email to **access@theartofservice.com** with this books' title in the subject to get the Knowledge assets Self Assessment Tool right away.

# Your feedback is invaluable to us

If you recently bought this book, we would love to hear from you! You can do this by writing a review on amazon (or the online store where you purchased this book) about your last purchase! As part of our continual service improvement process, we love to hear real client experiences and feedback.

**How does it work?**
To post a review on Amazon, just log in to your account and click on the Create Your Own Review button (under Customer Reviews) of the relevant product page. You can find examples of product reviews in Amazon. If you purchased from another online store, simply follow their procedures.

**What happens when I submit my review?**
Once you have submitted your review, send us an email at review@theartofservice.com with the link to your review so we can properly thank you for your feedback.

# Purpose of this Self-Assessment

This Self-Assessment has been developed to improve understanding of the requirements and elements of Knowledge assets, based on best practices and standards in business process architecture, design and quality management.

It is designed to allow for a rapid Self-Assessment to determine how closely existing management practices and procedures correspond to the elements of the Self-Assessment.

The criteria of requirements and elements of Knowledge assets have been rephrased in the format of a Self-Assessment questionnaire, with a seven-criterion scoring system, as explained in this document.

In this format, even with limited background knowledge of

Knowledge assets, a manager can quickly review existing operations to determine how they measure up to the standards. This in turn can serve as the starting point of a 'gap analysis' to identify management tools or system elements that might usefully be implemented in the organization to help improve overall performance.

# How to use the Self-Assessment

On the following pages are a series of questions to identify to what extent your Knowledge assets initiative is complete in comparison to the requirements set in standards.

To facilitate answering the questions, there is a space in front of each question to enter a score on a scale of '1' to '5'.

1 Strongly Disagree

2 Disagree

3 Neutral

4 Agree

5 Strongly Agree

*Read the question and rate it with the following in front of mind:*

**'In my belief,
the answer to this question is clearly defined'.**

There are two ways in which you can choose to interpret this statement;
1.  how aware are you that the answer to the question is clearly defined
2.  for more in-depth analysis you can choose to gather

evidence and confirm the answer to the question. This obviously will take more time, most Self-Assessment users opt for the first way to interpret the question and dig deeper later on based on the outcome of the overall Self-Assessment.

A score of '1' would mean that the answer is not clear at all, where a '5' would mean the answer is crystal clear and defined. Leave emtpy when the question is not applicable or you don't want to answer it, you can skip it without affecting your score. Write your score in the space provided.

After you have responded to all the appropriate statements in each section, compute your average score for that section, using the formula provided, and round to the nearest tenth. Then transfer to the corresponding spoke in the Knowledge assets Scorecard on the second next page of the Self-Assessment.

Your completed Knowledge assets Scorecard will give you a clear presentation of which Knowledge assets areas need attention.

# Knowledge assets
# Scorecard Example

Example of how the finalized Scorecard can look like:

# Knowledge assets
# Scorecard

Your Scores:

# BEGINNING OF THE SELF-ASSESSMENT:

# CRITERION #1: RECOGNIZE

INTENT: Be aware of the need for change. Recognize that there is an unfavorable variation, problem or symptom.

In my belief, the answer to this question is clearly defined:

5 Strongly Agree

4 Agree

3 Neutral

2 Disagree

1 Strongly Disagree

1. What should be considered when identifying available resources, constraints, and deadlines?
<--- Score

2. To what extent would your organization benefit from being recognized as a award recipient?
<--- Score

3. What extra resources will you need?

<--- Score

4. Consider your own knowledge assets project, what types of organizational problems do you think might be causing or affecting your problem, based on the work done so far?
<--- Score

5. What is the problem or issue?
<--- Score

6. How are you going to measure success?
<--- Score

7. What tools and technologies are needed for a custom knowledge assets project?
<--- Score

8. Do you have/need 24-hour access to key personnel?
<--- Score

9. What situation(s) led to this knowledge assets Self Assessment?
<--- Score

10. What do you need to start doing?
<--- Score

11. Will new equipment/products be required to facilitate knowledge assets delivery, for example is new software needed?
<--- Score

12. Will a response program recognize when a crisis occurs and provide some level of response?
<--- Score

13. Which information does the knowledge assets business case need to include?
<--- Score

14. Are there knowledge assets problems defined?
<--- Score

15. What are your needs in relation to knowledge assets skills, labor, equipment, and markets?
<--- Score

16. Does your organization need more knowledge assets education?
<--- Score

17. Are problem definition and motivation clearly presented?
<--- Score

18. Who needs to know about knowledge assets?
<--- Score

19. Will it solve real problems?
<--- Score

20. Who defines the rules in relation to any given issue?
<--- Score

21. Are there any revenue recognition issues?
<--- Score

22. Are you dealing with any of the same issues today as yesterday? What can you do about this?
<--- Score

23. Will knowledge assets deliverables need to be tested and, if so, by whom?
<--- Score

24. Are there any specific expectations or concerns about the knowledge assets team, knowledge assets itself?
<--- Score

25. Have you identified your knowledge assets key performance indicators?
<--- Score

26. What is the smallest subset of the problem you can usefully solve?
<--- Score

27. What are the stakeholder objectives to be achieved with knowledge assets?
<--- Score

28. How are the knowledge assets's objectives aligned to the group's overall stakeholder strategy?
<--- Score

29. What are the timeframes required to resolve each of the issues/problems?
<--- Score

30. Is the need for organizational change recognized?
<--- Score

31. Are controls defined to recognize and contain problems?
<--- Score

32. For your knowledge assets project, identify and describe the business environment, is there more than one layer to the business environment?
<--- Score

33. What is the knowledge assets problem definition? What do you need to resolve?
<--- Score

34. What needs to be done?
<--- Score

35. Does knowledge assets create potential expectations in other areas that need to be recognized and considered?
<--- Score

36. Think about the people you identified for your knowledge assets project and the project responsibilities you would assign to them, what kind of training do you think they would need to perform these responsibilities effectively?
<--- Score

37. Do you know what you need to know about knowledge assets?
<--- Score

38. How do you take a forward-looking perspective in identifying knowledge assets research related to market response and models?
<--- Score

39. How do you assess your knowledge assets workforce capability and capacity needs, including

skills, competencies, and staffing levels?
<--- Score

40. Are there recognized knowledge assets problems?
<--- Score

41. What does knowledge assets success mean to the stakeholders?
<--- Score

42. Are your goals realistic? Do you need to redefine your problem? Perhaps the problem has changed or maybe you have reached your goal and need to set a new one?
<--- Score

43. How can auditing be a preventative security measure?
<--- Score

44. What are the minority interests and what amount of minority interests can be recognized?
<--- Score

45. To what extent does each concerned units management team recognize knowledge assets as an effective investment?
<--- Score

46. Who are your key stakeholders who need to sign off?
<--- Score

47. Can management personnel recognize the monetary benefit of knowledge assets?
<--- Score

48. What are the expected benefits of knowledge assets to the stakeholder?
<--- Score

49. What information do users need?
<--- Score

50. Who else hopes to benefit from it?
<--- Score

51. How do you identify the kinds of information that you will need?
<--- Score

52. What activities does the governance board need to consider?
<--- Score

53. As a sponsor, customer or management, how important is it to meet goals, objectives?
<--- Score

54. How does it fit into your organizational needs and tasks?
<--- Score

55. Do you need different information or graphics?
<--- Score

56. Are employees recognized or rewarded for performance that demonstrates the highest levels of integrity?
<--- Score

57. How much are sponsors, customers, partners,

stakeholders involved in knowledge assets? In other words, what are the risks, if knowledge assets does not deliver successfully?
<--- Score

58. Looking at each person individually – does every one have the qualities which are needed to work in this group?
<--- Score

59. Do you need to avoid or amend any knowledge assets activities?
<--- Score

60. What prevents you from making the changes you know will make you a more effective knowledge assets leader?
<--- Score

61. What would happen if knowledge assets weren't done?
<--- Score

62. What problems are you facing and how do you consider knowledge assets will circumvent those obstacles?
<--- Score

63. Is it clear when you think of the day ahead of you what activities and tasks you need to complete?
<--- Score

64. What training and capacity building actions are needed to implement proposed reforms?
<--- Score

65. Who needs what information?
<--- Score

66. What else needs to be measured?
<--- Score

67. What vendors make products that address the knowledge assets needs?
<--- Score

68. When a knowledge assets manager recognizes a problem, what options are available?
<--- Score

Add up total points for this section:
_ _ _ _ _  = Total points for this section

Divided by: _ _ _ _ _ _  (number of statements answered) = _ _ _ _ _ _
Average score for this section

Transfer your score to the knowledge assets Index at the beginning of the Self-Assessment.

# CRITERION #2: DEFINE:

INTENT: Formulate the stakeholder problem. Define the problem, needs and objectives.

In my belief, the answer to this question is clearly defined:

5 Strongly Agree

4 Agree

3 Neutral

2 Disagree

1 Strongly Disagree

1. Is the improvement team aware of the different versions of a process: what they think it is vs. what it actually is vs. what it should be vs. what it could be?
<--- Score

2. Is there a completed SIPOC representation, describing the Suppliers, Inputs, Process, Outputs, and Customers?
<--- Score

3. Will team members regularly document their knowledge assets work?
<--- Score

4. Are task requirements clearly defined?
<--- Score

5. How have you defined all knowledge assets requirements first?
<--- Score

6. Is knowledge assets linked to key stakeholder goals and objectives?
<--- Score

7. Is scope creep really all bad news?
<--- Score

8. What scope to assess?
<--- Score

9. How do you manage scope?
<--- Score

10. How and when will the baselines be defined?
<--- Score

11. Has the direction changed at all during the course of knowledge assets? If so, when did it change and why?
<--- Score

12. Have all basic functions of knowledge assets been defined?
<--- Score

13. Are audit criteria, scope, frequency and methods defined?
<--- Score

14. Is the knowledge assets scope manageable?
<--- Score

15. Do you all define knowledge assets in the same way?
<--- Score

16. Do you have a knowledge assets success story or case study ready to tell and share?
<--- Score

17. Are accountability and ownership for knowledge assets clearly defined?
<--- Score

18. What is the scope of knowledge assets?
<--- Score

19. Is there a completed, verified, and validated high-level 'as is' (not 'should be' or 'could be') stakeholder process map?
<--- Score

20. Are there different segments of customers?
<--- Score

21. Is the team formed and are team leaders (Coaches and Management Leads) assigned?
<--- Score

22. What are the rough order estimates on cost

savings/opportunities that knowledge assets brings?
<--- Score

23. Is there any additional knowledge assets definition of success?
<--- Score

24. What system do you use for gathering knowledge assets information?
<--- Score

25. How can the value of knowledge assets be defined?
<--- Score

26. What are the core elements of the knowledge assets business case?
<--- Score

27. How often are the team meetings?
<--- Score

28. What key stakeholder process output measure(s) does knowledge assets leverage and how?
<--- Score

29. Are team charters developed?
<--- Score

30. How do you gather requirements?
<--- Score

31. Has/have the customer(s) been identified?
<--- Score

32. How would you define knowledge assets

leadership?
<--- Score

33. Will team members perform knowledge assets work when assigned and in a timely fashion?
<--- Score

34. Has a team charter been developed and communicated?
<--- Score

35. Has everyone on the team, including the team leaders, been properly trained?
<--- Score

36. What sort of initial information to gather?
<--- Score

37. What are the boundaries of the scope? What is in bounds and what is not? What is the start point? What is the stop point?
<--- Score

38. Is knowledge assets required?
<--- Score

39. Has a project plan, Gantt chart, or similar been developed/completed?
<--- Score

40. How do you gather knowledge assets requirements?
<--- Score

41. Are improvement team members fully trained on knowledge assets?

<--- Score

42. Who is gathering knowledge assets information?
<--- Score

43. Are customer(s) identified and segmented
according to their different needs and requirements?
<--- Score

44. Are stakeholder processes mapped?
<--- Score

45. How was the 'as is' process map developed,
reviewed, verified and validated?
<--- Score

46. Has a knowledge assets requirement not been
met?
<--- Score

47. Who is gathering information?
<--- Score

48. What are the tasks and definitions?
<--- Score

49. Where can you gather more information?
<--- Score

50. How do you gather the stories?
<--- Score

51. Does the team have regular meetings?
<--- Score

52. Are resources adequate for the scope?

<--- Score

53. What is out of scope?
<--- Score

54. What is the context?
<--- Score

55. What customer feedback methods were used to solicit their input?
<--- Score

56. Scope of sensitive information?
<--- Score

57. Is a fully trained team formed, supported, and committed to work on the knowledge assets improvements?
<--- Score

58. Is the team adequately staffed with the desired cross-functionality? If not, what additional resources are available to the team?
<--- Score

59. Have specific policy objectives been defined?
<--- Score

60. Has your scope been defined?
<--- Score

61. Have the customer needs been translated into specific, measurable requirements? How?
<--- Score

62. Is the current 'as is' process being followed? If not,

what are the discrepancies?
<--- Score

63. Is knowledge assets currently on schedule according to the plan?
<--- Score

64. What is in scope?
<--- Score

65. In what way can you redefine the criteria of choice clients have in your category in your favor?
<--- Score

66. Has the knowledge assets work been fairly and/ or equitably divided and delegated among team members who are qualified and capable to perform the work? Has everyone contributed?
<--- Score

67. Is there regularly 100% attendance at the team meetings? If not, have appointed substitutes attended to preserve cross-functionality and full representation?
<--- Score

68. Do the problem and goal statements meet the SMART criteria (specific, measurable, attainable, relevant, and time-bound)?
<--- Score

69. When is the estimated completion date?
<--- Score

70. Has a high-level 'as is' process map been completed, verified and validated?

<--- Score

71. What are the knowledge assets tasks and definitions?
<--- Score

72. Is data collected and displayed to better understand customer(s) critical needs and requirements.
<--- Score

73. What knowledge assets requirements should be gathered?
<--- Score

74. What constraints exist that might impact the team?
<--- Score

75. How are consistent knowledge assets definitions important?
<--- Score

76. How do you think the partners involved in knowledge assets would have defined success?
<--- Score

77. Are there any constraints known that bear on the ability to perform knowledge assets work? How is the team addressing them?
<--- Score

78. What is out-of-scope initially?
<--- Score

79. What is the scope?

<--- Score

80. Is there a knowledge assets management charter, including stakeholder case, problem and goal statements, scope, milestones, roles and responsibilities, communication plan?
<--- Score

81. What is the scope of the knowledge assets effort?
<--- Score

82. How do you manage changes in knowledge assets requirements?
<--- Score

83. What are the compelling stakeholder reasons for embarking on knowledge assets?
<--- Score

84. What sources do you use to gather information for a knowledge assets study?
<--- Score

85. Is it clearly defined in and to your organization what you do?
<--- Score

86. Has the improvement team collected the 'voice of the customer' (obtained feedback – qualitative and quantitative)?
<--- Score

87. What are the dynamics of the communication plan?
<--- Score

88. Is full participation by members in regularly held team meetings guaranteed?
<--- Score

89. Is there a clear knowledge assets case definition?
<--- Score

90. Is the scope of knowledge assets defined?
<--- Score

91. Who are the knowledge assets improvement team members, including Management Leads and Coaches?
<--- Score

92. How do you hand over knowledge assets context?
<--- Score

93. Is there a critical path to deliver knowledge assets results?
<--- Score

94. What are the record-keeping requirements of knowledge assets activities?
<--- Score

95. Does the scope remain the same?
<--- Score

96. Why are you doing knowledge assets and what is the scope?
<--- Score

97. What happens if knowledge assets's scope changes?
<--- Score

98. How do you keep key subject matter experts in the loop?
<--- Score

99. What would be the goal or target for a knowledge assets's improvement team?
<--- Score

100. What are the knowledge assets use cases?
<--- Score

101. Is the team sponsored by a champion or stakeholder leader?
<--- Score

102. Are approval levels defined for contracts and supplements to contracts?
<--- Score

103. Is special knowledge assets user knowledge required?
<--- Score

104. What defines best in class?
<--- Score

105. What is the definition of success?
<--- Score

106. What knowledge assets services do you require?
<--- Score

107. When are meeting minutes sent out? Who is on the distribution list?
<--- Score

108. How does the knowledge assets manager ensure against scope creep?
<--- Score

109. What intelligence can you gather?
<--- Score

110. Who defines (or who defined) the rules and roles?
<--- Score

111. What is in the scope and what is not in scope?
<--- Score

112. Are different versions of process maps needed to account for the different types of inputs?
<--- Score

113. Have all of the relationships been defined properly?
<--- Score

114. How will variation in the actual durations of each activity be dealt with to ensure that the expected knowledge assets results are met?
<--- Score

115. How is the team tracking and documenting its work?
<--- Score

116. What scope do you want your strategy to cover?
<--- Score

117. What was the context?
<--- Score

118. How do you catch knowledge assets definition inconsistencies?
<--- Score

119. If substitutes have been appointed, have they been briefed on the knowledge assets goals and received regular communications as to the progress to date?
<--- Score

120. What are the Roles and Responsibilities for each team member and its leadership? Where is this documented?
<--- Score

121. When is/was the knowledge assets start date?
<--- Score

122. What specifically is the problem? Where does it occur? When does it occur? What is its extent?
<--- Score

123. What critical content must be communicated – who, what, when, where, and how?
<--- Score

124. What is the worst case scenario?
<--- Score

125. Has anyone else (internal or external to the group) attempted to solve this problem or a similar one before? If so, what knowledge can be leveraged from these previous efforts?
<--- Score

126. How would you define the culture at your organization, how susceptible is it to knowledge assets changes?
<--- Score

127. How will the knowledge assets team and the group measure complete success of knowledge assets?
<--- Score

128. What baselines are required to be defined and managed?
<--- Score

129. What is the definition of knowledge assets excellence?
<--- Score

130. How did the knowledge assets manager receive input to the development of a knowledge assets improvement plan and the estimated completion dates/times of each activity?
<--- Score

131. How do you manage unclear knowledge assets requirements?
<--- Score

132. What information should you gather?
<--- Score

133. Will a knowledge assets production readiness review be required?
<--- Score

134. Is the knowledge assets scope complete and

appropriately sized?
<--- Score

135. What information do you gather?
<--- Score

136. Are roles and responsibilities formally defined?
<--- Score

137. Is the team equipped with available and reliable resources?
<--- Score

138. Are required metrics defined, what are they?
<--- Score

139. The political context: who holds power?
<--- Score

140. Are customers identified and high impact areas defined?
<--- Score

Add up total points for this section:
_ _ _ _ _ = Total points for this section

Divided by: _ _ _ _ _ _ (number of statements answered) = _ _ _ _ _ _
Average score for this section

Transfer your score to the knowledge assets Index at the beginning of the Self-Assessment.

# CRITERION #3: MEASURE:

INTENT: Gather the correct data. Measure the current performance and evolution of the situation.

In my belief, the answer to this question is clearly defined:

5 Strongly Agree

4 Agree

3 Neutral

2 Disagree

1 Strongly Disagree

1. Are indirect costs charged to the knowledge assets program?
<--- Score

2. Are the units of measure consistent?
<--- Score

3. What are the operational costs after knowledge assets deployment?

<--- Score

4. Have the concerns of stakeholders to help identify and define potential barriers been obtained and analyzed?
<--- Score

5. What are the current costs of the knowledge assets process?
<--- Score

6. What is the right balance of time and resources between investigation, analysis, and discussion and dissemination?
<--- Score

7. What would it cost to replace your technology?
<--- Score

8. Have you made assumptions about the shape of the future, particularly its impact on your customers and competitors?
<--- Score

9. How do you know that any knowledge assets analysis is complete and comprehensive?
<--- Score

10. How do you focus on what is right -not who is right?
<--- Score

11. What do people want to verify?
<--- Score

12. What does losing customers cost your

organization?
<--- Score

13. How are you verifying it?
<--- Score

14. How to cause the change?
<--- Score

15. How frequently do you track knowledge assets measures?
<--- Score

16. How do you verify and validate the knowledge assets data?
<--- Score

17. Was a life-cycle cost analysis performed?
<--- Score

18. What is an unallowable cost?
<--- Score

19. How do you identify and analyze stakeholders and their interests?
<--- Score

20. How do you verify knowledge assets completeness and accuracy?
<--- Score

21. Where is it measured?
<--- Score

22. What does verifying compliance entail?
<--- Score

23. How can you measure knowledge assets in a systematic way?
<--- Score

24. Is Process Variation Displayed/Communicated?
<--- Score

25. What data was collected (past, present, future/ongoing)?
<--- Score

26. How do you aggregate measures across priorities?
<--- Score

27. What evidence is there and what is measured?
<--- Score

28. What are the uncertainties surrounding estimates of impact?
<--- Score

29. Do you have any cost knowledge assets limitation requirements?
<--- Score

30. What is the total fixed cost?
<--- Score

31. What particular quality tools did the team find helpful in establishing measurements?
<--- Score

32. What is your decision requirements diagram?
<--- Score

33. How do you verify the authenticity of the data and information used?
<--- Score

34. How do you verify and develop ideas and innovations?
<--- Score

35. Are there any easy-to-implement alternatives to knowledge assets? Sometimes other solutions are available that do not require the cost implications of a full-blown project?
<--- Score

36. What drives O&M cost?
<--- Score

37. How do you do risk analysis of rare, cascading, catastrophic events?
<--- Score

38. Have design-to-cost goals been established?
<--- Score

39. What are your customers expectations and measures?
<--- Score

40. Do you have a flow diagram of what happens?
<--- Score

41. Which measures and indicators matter?
<--- Score

42. Is the solution cost-effective?
<--- Score

43. What causes extra work or rework?
<--- Score

44. Among the knowledge assets product and service cost to be estimated, which is considered hardest to estimate?
<--- Score

45. What do you measure and why?
<--- Score

46. What would be a real cause for concern?
<--- Score

47. How do you measure variability?
<--- Score

48. Do you verify that corrective actions were taken?
<--- Score

49. What could cause delays in the schedule?
<--- Score

50. What are the key input variables? What are the key process variables? What are the key output variables?
<--- Score

51. How do you verify performance?
<--- Score

52. Does the knowledge assets task fit the client's priorities?
<--- Score

53. What are the costs of reform?

<--- Score

54. Does knowledge assets analysis show the relationships among important knowledge assets factors?
<--- Score

55. How do you quantify and qualify impacts?
<--- Score

56. Was a business case (cost/benefit) developed?
<--- Score

57. What disadvantage does this cause for the user?
<--- Score

58. What causes mismanagement?
<--- Score

59. How will measures be used to manage and adapt?
<--- Score

60. Do you effectively measure and reward individual and team performance?
<--- Score

61. How do your measurements capture actionable knowledge assets information for use in exceeding your customers expectations and securing your customers engagement?
<--- Score

62. Was a data collection plan established?
<--- Score

63. Have you included everything in your knowledge

assets cost models?
<--- Score

64. What measurements are possible, practicable and meaningful?
<--- Score

65. The approach of traditional knowledge assets works for detail complexity but is focused on a systematic approach rather than an understanding of the nature of systems themselves, what approach will permit your organization to deal with the kind of unpredictable emergent behaviors that dynamic complexity can introduce?
<--- Score

66. What key measures identified indicate the performance of the stakeholder process?
<--- Score

67. How will success or failure be measured?
<--- Score

68. What are the knowledge assets key cost drivers?
<--- Score

69. How are costs allocated?
<--- Score

70. Are process variation components displayed/communicated using suitable charts, graphs, plots?
<--- Score

71. Is a follow-up focused external knowledge assets review required?
<--- Score

72. How do you measure success?
<--- Score

73. How will effects be measured?
<--- Score

74. What are the estimated costs of proposed changes?
<--- Score

75. Is data collected on key measures that were identified?
<--- Score

76. Who participated in the data collection for measurements?
<--- Score

77. Are supply costs steady or fluctuating?
<--- Score

78. Is there a Performance Baseline?
<--- Score

79. How can you reduce costs?
<--- Score

80. How are measurements made?
<--- Score

81. Have changes been properly/adequately analyzed for effect?
<--- Score

82. Are you aware of what could cause a problem?

<--- Score

83. What can be used to verify compliance?
<--- Score

84. When is Root Cause Analysis Required?
<--- Score

85. What happens if cost savings do not materialize?
<--- Score

86. Are key measures identified and agreed upon?
<--- Score

87. Will knowledge assets have an impact on current business continuity, disaster recovery processes and/ or infrastructure?
<--- Score

88. Is the scope of knowledge assets cost analysis cost-effective?
<--- Score

89. Are actual costs in line with budgeted costs?
<--- Score

90. Who should receive measurement reports?
<--- Score

91. What does a Test Case verify?
<--- Score

92. How will you measure your knowledge assets effectiveness?
<--- Score

93. Is there an opportunity to verify requirements?
<--- Score

94. What are your primary costs, revenues, assets?
<--- Score

95. What harm might be caused?
<--- Score

96. How do you verify the knowledge assets requirements quality?
<--- Score

97. When are costs are incurred?
<--- Score

98. What are the agreed upon definitions of the high impact areas, defect(s), unit(s), and opportunities that will figure into the process capability metrics?
<--- Score

99. How is progress measured?
<--- Score

100. What kind of analytics data will be gathered?
<--- Score

101. What is the total cost related to deploying knowledge assets, including any consulting or professional services?
<--- Score

102. Are you taking your company in the direction of better and revenue or cheaper and cost?
<--- Score

103. How do you prevent mis-estimating cost?
<--- Score

104. How will your organization measure success?
<--- Score

105. What has the team done to assure the stability
and accuracy of the measurement process?
<--- Score

106. Why do you expend time and effort to
implement measurement, for whom?
<--- Score

107. Are missed knowledge assets opportunities
costing your organization money?
<--- Score

108. What are your key knowledge assets indicators
that you will measure, analyze and track?
<--- Score

109. How can you reduce the costs of obtaining
inputs?
<--- Score

110. How will costs be allocated?
<--- Score

111. What methods are feasible and acceptable to
estimate the impact of reforms?
<--- Score

112. What is your knowledge assets quality cost
segregation study?
<--- Score

113. How will you measure success?
<--- Score

114. How do you control the overall costs of your work processes?
<--- Score

115. How do you measure efficient delivery of knowledge assets services?
<--- Score

116. What causes investor action?
<--- Score

117. Are the measurements objective?
<--- Score

118. What charts has the team used to display the components of variation in the process?
<--- Score

119. Is key measure data collection planned and executed, process variation displayed and communicated and performance baselined?
<--- Score

120. Is it possible to estimate the impact of unanticipated complexity such as wrong or failed assumptions, feedback, etcetera on proposed reforms?
<--- Score

121. What are the costs and benefits?
<--- Score

122. Does knowledge assets systematically track and analyze outcomes for accountability and quality improvement?
<--- Score

123. How do you verify your resources?
<--- Score

124. How can you measure the performance?
<--- Score

125. Does knowledge assets analysis isolate the fundamental causes of problems?
<--- Score

126. Can you measure the return on analysis?
<--- Score

127. Which costs should be taken into account?
<--- Score

128. How large is the gap between current performance and the customer-specified (goal) performance?
<--- Score

129. Have all non-recommended alternatives been analyzed in sufficient detail?
<--- Score

130. Are there measurements based on task performance?
<--- Score

131. Has a cost benefit analysis been performed?
<--- Score

132. Have the types of risks that may impact knowledge assets been identified and analyzed?
<--- Score

133. Do staff have the necessary skills to collect, analyze, and report data?
<--- Score

134. What is measured? Why?
<--- Score

135. How much does it cost?
<--- Score

136. What are the types and number of measures to use?
<--- Score

137. At what cost?
<--- Score

138. Have you found any 'ground fruit' or 'low-hanging fruit' for immediate remedies to the gap in performance?
<--- Score

139. What are your key knowledge assets organizational performance measures, including key short and longer-term financial measures?
<--- Score

140. How sensitive must the knowledge assets strategy be to cost?
<--- Score

141. Who is involved in verifying compliance?
<--- Score

142. Are losses documented, analyzed, and remedial processes developed to prevent future losses?
<--- Score

143. Are the knowledge assets benefits worth its costs?
<--- Score

144. Which stakeholder characteristics are analyzed?
<--- Score

145. Can you do knowledge assets without complex (expensive) analysis?
<--- Score

146. Did you tackle the cause or the symptom?
<--- Score

147. What causes innovation to fail or succeed in your organization?
<--- Score

148. What measurements are being captured?
<--- Score

149. What does your operating model cost?
<--- Score

150. Are high impact defects defined and identified in the stakeholder process?
<--- Score

151. How is performance measured?

<--- Score

152. How can you manage cost down?
<--- Score

153. Why do the measurements/indicators matter?
<--- Score

154. How do you measure lifecycle phases?
<--- Score

155. Does a knowledge assets quantification method exist?
<--- Score

156. Where can you go to verify the info?
<--- Score

157. What are the costs of delaying knowledge assets action?
<--- Score

158. How does cost-to-serve analysis help?
<--- Score

159. What potential environmental factors impact the knowledge assets effort?
<--- Score

160. How is the value delivered by knowledge assets being measured?
<--- Score

161. Are there competing knowledge assets priorities?
<--- Score

162. Is the cost worth the knowledge assets effort ?
<--- Score

163. Is a solid data collection plan established that includes measurement systems analysis?
<--- Score

164. How do you verify if knowledge assets is built right?
<--- Score

165. Do the benefits outweigh the costs?
<--- Score

166. Is data collection planned and executed?
<--- Score

167. What tests verify requirements?
<--- Score

168. Are you able to realize any cost savings?
<--- Score

169. When a disaster occurs, who gets priority?
<--- Score

170. How can a knowledge assets test verify your ideas or assumptions?
<--- Score

171. When should you bother with diagrams?
<--- Score

172. What are your operating costs?
<--- Score

173. Do you aggressively reward and promote the people who have the biggest impact on creating excellent knowledge assets services/products?
<--- Score

174. Does your organization systematically track and analyze outcomes related for accountability and quality improvement?
<--- Score

175. What is the cost of rework?
<--- Score

176. What are allowable costs?
<--- Score

177. Has a cost center been established?
<--- Score

178. Is long term and short term variability accounted for?
<--- Score

179. What relevant entities could be measured?
<--- Score

180. How frequently do you verify your knowledge assets strategy?
<--- Score

181. What are you verifying?
<--- Score

182. What could cause you to change course?
<--- Score

183. How do you stay flexible and focused to recognize larger knowledge assets results?
<--- Score

184. What is your cost benefit analysis?
<--- Score

Add up total points for this section:
_____ = Total points for this section

Divided by: _____ (number of statements answered) = _____
Average score for this section

Transfer your score to the knowledge assets Index at the beginning of the Self-Assessment.

# CRITERION #4: ANALYZE:

INTENT: Analyze causes, assumptions and hypotheses.

In my belief, the answer to this question is clearly defined:

5 Strongly Agree

4 Agree

3 Neutral

2 Disagree

1 Strongly Disagree

1. What is the output?
<--- Score

2. Are knowledge assets changes recognized early enough to be approved through the regular process?
<--- Score

3. How has the knowledge assets data been gathered?
<--- Score

4. What are the revised rough estimates of the financial savings/opportunity for knowledge assets improvements?
<--- Score

5. A compounding model resolution with available relevant data can often provide insight towards a solution methodology; which knowledge assets models, tools and techniques are necessary?
<--- Score

6. Are all team members qualified for all tasks?
<--- Score

7. Think about some of the processes you undertake within your organization, which do you own?
<--- Score

8. Where is the data coming from to measure compliance?
<--- Score

9. Where is knowledge assets data gathered?
<--- Score

10. What is the cost of poor quality as supported by the team's analysis?
<--- Score

11. What methods do you use to gather knowledge assets data?
<--- Score

12. Do several people in different organizational units assist with the knowledge assets process?
<--- Score

13. How do you implement and manage your work processes to ensure that they meet design requirements?
<--- Score

14. Can you add value to the current knowledge assets decision-making process (largely qualitative) by incorporating uncertainty modeling (more quantitative)?
<--- Score

15. What are your outputs?
<--- Score

16. Do you have the authority to produce the output?
<--- Score

17. What are the personnel training and qualifications required?
<--- Score

18. How do you identify specific knowledge assets investment opportunities and emerging trends?
<--- Score

19. Was a detailed process map created to amplify critical steps of the 'as is' stakeholder process?
<--- Score

20. What conclusions were drawn from the team's data collection and analysis? How did the team reach these conclusions?
<--- Score

21. Do your employees have the opportunity to do

what they do best everyday?
<--- Score

22. What is the complexity of the output produced?
<--- Score

23. Record-keeping requirements flow from the records needed as inputs, outputs, controls and for transformation of a knowledge assets process, are the records needed as inputs to the knowledge assets process available?
<--- Score

24. How do you promote understanding that opportunity for improvement is not criticism of the status quo, or the people who created the status quo?
<--- Score

25. What is your organizations system for selecting qualified vendors?
<--- Score

26. Is the knowledge assets process severely broken such that a re-design is necessary?
<--- Score

27. Is the performance gap determined?
<--- Score

28. What are evaluation criteria for the output?
<--- Score

29. How was the detailed process map generated, verified, and validated?
<--- Score

30. Is the gap/opportunity displayed and communicated in financial terms?
<--- Score

31. What are the necessary qualifications?
<--- Score

32. What do you need to qualify?
<--- Score

33. How do mission and objectives affect the knowledge assets processes of your organization?
<--- Score

34. What other organizational variables, such as reward systems or communication systems, affect the performance of this knowledge assets process?
<--- Score

35. Are all staff in core knowledge assets subjects Highly Qualified?
<--- Score

36. How do your work systems and key work processes relate to and capitalize on your core competencies?
<--- Score

37. Have the problem and goal statements been updated to reflect the additional knowledge gained from the analyze phase?
<--- Score

38. What other jobs or tasks affect the performance of the steps in the knowledge assets process?
<--- Score

39. Were Pareto charts (or similar) used to portray the 'heavy hitters' (or key sources of variation)?
<--- Score

40. What are the disruptive knowledge assets technologies that enable your organization to radically change your business processes?
<--- Score

41. What data do you need to collect?
<--- Score

42. What are your current levels and trends in key knowledge assets measures or indicators of product and process performance that are important to and directly serve your customers?
<--- Score

43. What are your knowledge assets processes?
<--- Score

44. How is the knowledge assets Value Stream Mapping managed?
<--- Score

45. What resources go in to get the desired output?
<--- Score

46. How difficult is it to qualify what knowledge assets ROI is?
<--- Score

47. How does the organization define, manage, and improve its knowledge assets processes?
<--- Score

48. Has an output goal been set?
<--- Score

49. How is knowledge assets data gathered?
<--- Score

50. Did any value-added analysis or 'lean thinking'
take place to identify some of the gaps shown on the
'as is' process map?
<--- Score

51. Should you invest in industry-recognized
qualifications?
<--- Score

52. How often will data be collected for measures?
<--- Score

**53. What technologies or processes are used
to ensure secure access to your organizations
knowledge assets?**
<--- Score

54. How are outputs preserved and protected?
<--- Score

55. Are gaps between current performance and the
goal performance identified?
<--- Score

56. Think about the functions involved in your
knowledge assets project, what processes flow from
these functions?
<--- Score

57. What will drive knowledge assets change?
<--- Score

58. What knowledge assets metrics are outputs of the process?
<--- Score

59. Is data and process analysis, root cause analysis and quantifying the gap/opportunity in place?
<--- Score

60. What are your best practices for minimizing knowledge assets project risk, while demonstrating incremental value and quick wins throughout the knowledge assets project lifecycle?
<--- Score

61. Who will gather what data?
<--- Score

62. What qualifies as competition?
<--- Score

63. What output to create?
<--- Score

64. What does the data say about the performance of the stakeholder process?
<--- Score

65. Identify an operational issue in your organization, for example, could a particular task be done more quickly or more efficiently by knowledge assets?
<--- Score

66. Was a cause-and-effect diagram used to explore

the different types of causes (or sources of variation)?
<--- Score

67. Who gets your output?
<--- Score

68. How do you define collaboration and team output?
<--- Score

69. Is pre-qualification of suppliers carried out?
<--- Score

70. Who is involved with workflow mapping?
<--- Score

71. How many input/output points does it require?
<--- Score

72. Is the required knowledge assets data gathered?
<--- Score

73. What data is gathered?
<--- Score

74. How do you use knowledge assets data and information to support organizational decision making and innovation?
<--- Score

75. What quality tools were used to get through the analyze phase?
<--- Score

76. What qualifications are necessary?
<--- Score

77. What are the best opportunities for value improvement?
<--- Score

78. Do your contracts/agreements contain data security obligations?
<--- Score

79. What are your key performance measures or indicators and in-process measures for the control and improvement of your knowledge assets processes?
<--- Score

80. What training and qualifications will you need?
<--- Score

81. What knowledge assets data do you gather or use now?
<--- Score

82. Have any additional benefits been identified that will result from closing all or most of the gaps?
<--- Score

83. Do you, as a leader, bounce back quickly from setbacks?
<--- Score

84. What were the financial benefits resulting from any 'ground fruit or low-hanging fruit' (quick fixes)?
<--- Score

85. What qualifications and skills do you need?
<--- Score

86. Is the suppliers process defined and controlled?
<--- Score

87. How do you measure the operational performance of your key work systems and processes, including productivity, cycle time, and other appropriate measures of process effectiveness, efficiency, and innovation?
<--- Score

88. Were there any improvement opportunities identified from the process analysis?
<--- Score

89. What successful thing are you doing today that may be blinding you to new growth opportunities?
<--- Score

90. Has data output been validated?
<--- Score

91. Have you defined which data is gathered how?
<--- Score

92. Are your outputs consistent?
<--- Score

93. What process should you select for improvement?
<--- Score

94. How is the data gathered?
<--- Score

95. What kind of crime could a potential new hire have committed that would not only not disqualify him/her from being hired by your organization,

but would actually indicate that he/she might be a particularly good fit?
<--- Score

96. What is the Value Stream Mapping?
<--- Score

97. What qualifications do knowledge assets leaders need?
<--- Score

98. What information qualified as important?
<--- Score

99. An organizationally feasible system request is one that considers the mission, goals and objectives of the organization, key questions are: is the knowledge assets solution request practical and will it solve a problem or take advantage of an opportunity to achieve company goals?
<--- Score

100. Do staff qualifications match your project?
<--- Score

101. What tools were used to generate the list of possible causes?
<--- Score

102. Is the final output clearly identified?
<--- Score

103. What tools were used to narrow the list of possible causes?
<--- Score

104. Were any designed experiments used to generate additional insight into the data analysis?
<--- Score

105. Where can you get qualified talent today?
<--- Score

106. What did the team gain from developing a sub-process map?
<--- Score

107. What were the crucial 'moments of truth' on the process map?
<--- Score

108. How is the way you as the leader think and process information affecting your organizational culture?
<--- Score

109. Who qualifies to gain access to data?
<--- Score

110. Did any additional data need to be collected?
<--- Score

111. What qualifications are needed?
<--- Score

112. What is your organizations process which leads to recognition of value generation?
<--- Score

113. What controls do you have in place to protect data?
<--- Score

114. Do your leaders quickly bounce back from setbacks?
<--- Score

115. What are your current levels and trends in key measures or indicators of knowledge assets product and process performance that are important to and directly serve your customers? How do these results compare with the performance of your competitors and other organizations with similar offerings?
<--- Score

Add up total points for this section:
_ _ _ _ _  = Total points for this section

Divided by: _ _ _ _ _ _  (number of statements answered) =  _ _ _ _ _ _
Average score for this section

Transfer your score to the knowledge assets Index at the beginning of the Self-Assessment.

# CRITERION #5: IMPROVE:

INTENT: Develop a practical solution.
Innovate, establish and test the
solution and to measure the results.

In my belief, the answer to this
question is clearly defined:

5 Strongly Agree

4 Agree

3 Neutral

2 Disagree

1 Strongly Disagree

1. Can the solution be designed and implemented within an acceptable time period?
<--- Score

2. Do you cover the five essential competencies: Communication, Collaboration,Innovation, Adaptability, and Leadership that improve an organizations ability to leverage the new knowledge assets in a volatile global economy?

<--- Score

3. Is there a small-scale pilot for proposed improvement(s)? What conclusions were drawn from the outcomes of a pilot?
<--- Score

4. What actually has to improve and by how much?
<--- Score

5. Who controls key decisions that will be made?
<--- Score

6. Which of the recognised risks out of all risks can be most likely transferred?
<--- Score

7. Does the goal represent a desired result that can be measured?
<--- Score

8. How do you go about comparing knowledge assets approaches/solutions?
<--- Score

9. How will you measure the results?
<--- Score

10. What tools were used to evaluate the potential solutions?
<--- Score

11. Explorations of the frontiers of knowledge assets will help you build influence, improve knowledge assets, optimize decision making, and sustain change, what is your approach?

<--- Score

12. How significant is the improvement in the eyes of the end user?
<--- Score

13. When you map the key players in your own work and the types/domains of relationships with them, which relationships do you find easy and which challenging, and why?
<--- Score

14. Do those selected for the knowledge assets team have a good general understanding of what knowledge assets is all about?
<--- Score

15. Who will be using the results of the measurement activities?
<--- Score

16. Are risk triggers captured?
<--- Score

17. Are the best solutions selected?
<--- Score

18. How will you know when its improved?
<--- Score

19. Is there a cost/benefit analysis of optimal solution(s)?
<--- Score

20. How can skill-level changes improve knowledge assets?

<--- Score

21. How do you improve knowledge assets service perception, and satisfaction?
<--- Score

22. Is supporting knowledge assets documentation required?
<--- Score

23. How are policy decisions made and where?
<--- Score

24. Are possible solutions generated and tested?
<--- Score

25. Are you assessing knowledge assets and risk?
<--- Score

26. How do you manage and improve your knowledge assets work systems to deliver customer value and achieve organizational success and sustainability?
<--- Score

27. Were any criteria developed to assist the team in testing and evaluating potential solutions?
<--- Score

28. What should a proof of concept or pilot accomplish?
<--- Score

29. What do you want to improve?
<--- Score

30. Is pilot data collected and analyzed?
<--- Score

31. Why improve in the first place?
<--- Score

32. Is the scope clearly documented?
<--- Score

33. What is knowledge assets's impact on utilizing the best solution(s)?
<--- Score

34. What communications are necessary to support the implementation of the solution?
<--- Score

35. What is the knowledge assets's sustainability risk?
<--- Score

36. How do you measure improved knowledge assets service perception, and satisfaction?
<--- Score

37. What tools were used to tap into the creativity and encourage 'outside the box' thinking?
<--- Score

38. What lessons, if any, from a pilot were incorporated into the design of the full-scale solution?
<--- Score

39. How do you link measurement and risk?
<--- Score

40. For estimation problems, how do you develop an

estimation statement?
<--- Score

41. What are your current levels and trends in key measures or indicators of workforce and leader development?
<--- Score

42. Is the solution technically practical?
<--- Score

43. Are there any constraints (technical, political, cultural, or otherwise) that would inhibit certain solutions?
<--- Score

44. What tools were most useful during the improve phase?
<--- Score

45. Can you identify any significant risks or exposures to knowledge assets third- parties (vendors, service providers, alliance partners etc) that concern you?
<--- Score

46. What are the implications of the one critical knowledge assets decision 10 minutes, 10 months, and 10 years from now?
<--- Score

47. What resources are required for the improvement efforts?
<--- Score

48. What does the 'should be' process map/design look like?

<--- Score

49. Have you identified breakpoints and/or risk tolerances that will trigger broad consideration of a potential need for intervention or modification of strategy?
<--- Score

50. For decision problems, how do you develop a decision statement?
<--- Score

51. Who will be responsible for making the decisions to include or exclude requested changes once knowledge assets is underway?
<--- Score

52. How do the knowledge assets results compare with the performance of your competitors and other organizations with similar offerings?
<--- Score

53. Risk events: what are the things that could go wrong?
<--- Score

54. Does a good decision guarantee a good outcome?
<--- Score

55. How will the group know that the solution worked?
<--- Score

56. What to do with the results or outcomes of measurements?
<--- Score

57. How do you improve your likelihood of success ?
<--- Score

58. What is the implementation plan?
<--- Score

59. What were the underlying assumptions on the cost-benefit analysis?
<--- Score

60. What can you do to improve?
<--- Score

61. How did the team generate the list of possible solutions?
<--- Score

62. Who controls the risk?
<--- Score

63. Are improved process ('should be') maps modified based on pilot data and analysis?
<--- Score

64. Who do you report knowledge assets results to?
<--- Score

65. Are decisions made in a timely manner?
<--- Score

66. What tools do you use once you have decided on a knowledge assets strategy and more importantly how do you choose?
<--- Score

67. Is the measure of success for knowledge assets understandable to a variety of people?
<--- Score

68. Is there a high likelihood that any recommendations will achieve their intended results?
<--- Score

69. How risky is your organization?
<--- Score

70. What went well, what should change, what can improve?
<--- Score

71. How do you define the solutions' scope?
<--- Score

72. How do you measure risk?
<--- Score

73. If you could go back in time five years, what decision would you make differently? What is your best guess as to what decision you're making today you might regret five years from now?
<--- Score

74. Who are the people involved in developing and implementing knowledge assets?
<--- Score

75. Is the optimal solution selected based on testing and analysis?
<--- Score

76. What attendant changes will need to be made to

ensure that the solution is successful?
<--- Score

77. Is a solution implementation plan established,
including schedule/work breakdown structure,
resources, risk management plan, cost/budget, and
control plan?
<--- Score

78. Risk factors: what are the characteristics of
knowledge assets that make it risky?
<--- Score

79. At what point will vulnerability assessments
be performed once knowledge assets is put into
production (e.g., ongoing Risk Management after
implementation)?
<--- Score

80. Risk Identification: What are the possible
risk events your organization faces in relation to
knowledge assets?
<--- Score

81. How will you know that a change is an
improvement?
<--- Score

82. knowledge assets risk decisions: whose call Is It?
<--- Score

83. Was a pilot designed for the proposed solution(s)?
<--- Score

84. How can you improve performance?
<--- Score

85. What is the risk?
<--- Score

86. Who makes the knowledge assets decisions in your organization?
<--- Score

87. Describe the design of the pilot and what tests were conducted, if any?
<--- Score

88. How can you improve knowledge assets?
<--- Score

89. Is the implementation plan designed?
<--- Score

90. What is the team's contingency plan for potential problems occurring in implementation?
<--- Score

91. To what extent does management recognize knowledge assets as a tool to increase the results?
<--- Score

92. How does the team improve its work?
<--- Score

93. What improvements have been achieved?
<--- Score

94. Do you combine technical expertise with business knowledge and knowledge assets Key topics include lifecycles, development approaches, requirements and how to make a business case?

<--- Score

95. What error proofing will be done to address some of the discrepancies observed in the 'as is' process?
<--- Score

96. What needs improvement? Why?
<--- Score

97. Are new and improved process ('should be') maps developed?
<--- Score

98. How do you keep improving knowledge assets?
<--- Score

99. How will the team or the process owner(s) monitor the implementation plan to see that it is working as intended?
<--- Score

100. How will you know that you have improved?
<--- Score

101. Will the controls trigger any other risks?
<--- Score

102. How does the solution remove the key sources of issues discovered in the analyze phase?
<--- Score

103. Was a knowledge assets charter developed?
<--- Score

104. How do you measure progress and evaluate training effectiveness?

<--- Score

105. Who will be responsible for documenting the knowledge assets requirements in detail?
<--- Score

106. Is a contingency plan established?
<--- Score

107. What is the magnitude of the improvements?
<--- Score

108. How do you decide how much to remunerate an employee?
<--- Score

109. What practices helps your organization to develop its capacity to recognize patterns?
<--- Score

110. In the past few months, what is the smallest change you have made that has had the biggest positive result? What was it about that small change that produced the large return?
<--- Score

111. How do you improve productivity?
<--- Score

Add up total points for this section:
_ _ _ _ _  = Total points for this section

Divided by: _ _ _ _ _ _ (number of statements answered) = _ _ _ _ _ _
Average score for this section

Transfer your score to the knowledge
assets Index at the beginning of the
Self-Assessment.

# CRITERION #6: CONTROL:

INTENT: Implement the practical solution. Maintain the performance and correct possible complications.

In my belief, the answer to this question is clearly defined:

5 Strongly Agree

4 Agree

3 Neutral

2 Disagree

1 Strongly Disagree

1. Who is the knowledge assets process owner?
<--- Score

2. Does knowledge assets appropriately measure and monitor risk?
<--- Score

3. How will you measure your QA plan's effectiveness?
<--- Score

4. How do you establish and deploy modified action plans if circumstances require a shift in plans and rapid execution of new plans?
<--- Score

5. What adjustments to the strategies are needed?
<--- Score

6. Is there a standardized process?
<--- Score

7. How can you best use all of your knowledge repositories to enhance learning and sharing?
<--- Score

8. What key inputs and outputs are being measured on an ongoing basis?
<--- Score

9. Will existing staff require re-training, for example, to learn new business processes?
<--- Score

10. Have new or revised work instructions resulted?
<--- Score

11. Is there a knowledge assets Communication plan covering who needs to get what information when?
<--- Score

12. What are the critical parameters to watch?
<--- Score

13. Are the planned controls in place?
<--- Score

14. Is knowledge gained on process shared and institutionalized?
<--- Score

15. Who is going to spread your message?
<--- Score

16. How might the group capture best practices and lessons learned so as to leverage improvements?
<--- Score

17. Is new knowledge gained imbedded in the response plan?
<--- Score

18. What other areas of the group might benefit from the knowledge assets team's improvements, knowledge, and learning?
<--- Score

19. How do controls support value?
<--- Score

20. How likely is the current knowledge assets plan to come in on schedule or on budget?
<--- Score

21. How will knowledge assets decisions be made and monitored?
<--- Score

22. You may have created your quality measures at a time when you lacked resources, technology wasn't up to the required standard, or low service levels were the industry norm. Have those circumstances

changed?

<--- Score

23. How will report readings be checked to effectively monitor performance?

<--- Score

24. How do you plan on providing proper recognition and disclosure of supporting companies?

<--- Score

25. Are controls in place and consistently applied?

<--- Score

26. What are you attempting to measure/monitor?

<--- Score

27. Are the planned controls working?

<--- Score

28. How do you select, collect, align, and integrate knowledge assets data and information for tracking daily operations and overall organizational performance, including progress relative to strategic objectives and action plans?

<--- Score

29. What other systems, operations, processes, and infrastructures (hiring practices, staffing, training, incentives/rewards, metrics/dashboards/scorecards, etc.) need updates, additions, changes, or deletions in order to facilitate knowledge transfer and improvements?

<--- Score

30. Is a response plan in place for when the input,

process, or output measures indicate an 'out-of-control' condition?
<--- Score

31. Do you monitor the effectiveness of your knowledge assets activities?
<--- Score

32. Is the knowledge assets test/monitoring cost justified?
<--- Score

33. Will the team be available to assist members in planning investigations?
<--- Score

34. What should the next improvement project be that is related to knowledge assets?
<--- Score

35. How will input, process, and output variables be checked to detect for sub-optimal conditions?
<--- Score

36. Who has control over resources?
<--- Score

37. What are the known security controls?
<--- Score

38. How do you monitor usage and cost?
<--- Score

39. Who controls critical resources?
<--- Score

40. What are your results for key measures or indicators of the accomplishment of your knowledge assets strategy and action plans, including building and strengthening core competencies?
<--- Score

41. How do your controls stack up?
<--- Score

42. Do you monitor the knowledge assets decisions made and fine tune them as they evolve?
<--- Score

43. What is the best design framework for knowledge assets organization now that, in a post industrial-age if the top-down, command and control model is no longer relevant?
<--- Score

44. How is change control managed?
<--- Score

45. What should you measure to verify efficiency gains?
<--- Score

46. How do you encourage people to take control and responsibility?
<--- Score

47. Is there a control plan in place for sustaining improvements (short and long-term)?
<--- Score

48. How do you spread information?
<--- Score

49. Does the knowledge assets performance meet the customer's requirements?
<--- Score

50. Are suggested corrective/restorative actions indicated on the response plan for known causes to problems that might surface?
<--- Score

51. Will your goals reflect your program budget?
<--- Score

52. Is there documentation that will support the successful operation of the improvement?
<--- Score

53. What quality tools were useful in the control phase?
<--- Score

54. Against what alternative is success being measured?
<--- Score

55. Can support from partners be adjusted?
<--- Score

56. Are new process steps, standards, and documentation ingrained into normal operations?
<--- Score

57. Has the improved process and its steps been standardized?
<--- Score

58. What is the recommended frequency of auditing?
<--- Score

59. What can you control?
<--- Score

60. Will any special training be provided for results interpretation?
<--- Score

61. Does a troubleshooting guide exist or is it needed?
<--- Score

62. How do senior leaders actions reflect a commitment to the organizations knowledge assets values?
<--- Score

63. How will the day-to-day responsibilities for monitoring and continual improvement be transferred from the improvement team to the process owner?
<--- Score

64. Is there an action plan in case of emergencies?
<--- Score

65. How will the process owner verify improvement in present and future sigma levels, process capabilities?
<--- Score

66. Is reporting being used or needed?
<--- Score

67. Are you measuring, monitoring and predicting knowledge assets activities to optimize operations

and profitability, and enhancing outcomes?
<--- Score

68. Can you adapt and adjust to changing knowledge assets situations?
<--- Score

69. What is the control/monitoring plan?
<--- Score

70. Who will be in control?
<--- Score

71. Are pertinent alerts monitored, analyzed and distributed to appropriate personnel?
<--- Score

72. What do your reports reflect?
<--- Score

73. Is there a transfer of ownership and knowledge to process owner and process team tasked with the responsibilities.
<--- Score

74. Is there a documented and implemented monitoring plan?
<--- Score

75. Where do ideas that reach policy makers and planners as proposals for knowledge assets strengthening and reform actually originate?
<--- Score

76. Are there documented procedures?
<--- Score

77. Has the knowledge assets value of standards been quantified?
<--- Score

78. What do you stand for--and what are you against?
<--- Score

79. Act/Adjust: What Do you Need to Do Differently?
<--- Score

80. Are operating procedures consistent?
<--- Score

81. Is there a recommended audit plan for routine surveillance inspections of knowledge assets's gains?
<--- Score

82. How widespread is its use?
<--- Score

83. Who sets the knowledge assets standards?
<--- Score

84. How will new or emerging customer needs/requirements be checked/communicated to orient the process toward meeting the new specifications and continually reducing variation?
<--- Score

85. Implementation Planning: is a pilot needed to test the changes before a full roll out occurs?
<--- Score

86. Do the knowledge assets decisions you make today help people and the planet tomorrow?

<--- Score

87. Is a response plan established and deployed?
<--- Score

88. Does job training on the documented procedures need to be part of the process team's education and training?
<--- Score

89. What is your theory of human motivation, and how does your compensation plan fit with that view?
<--- Score

90. What are the key elements of your knowledge assets performance improvement system, including your evaluation, organizational learning, and innovation processes?
<--- Score

91. How is knowledge assets project cost planned, managed, monitored?
<--- Score

92. How will the process owner and team be able to hold the gains?
<--- Score

93. In the case of a knowledge assets project, the criteria for the audit derive from implementation objectives, an audit of a knowledge assets project involves assessing whether the recommendations outlined for implementation have been met, can you track that any knowledge assets project is implemented as planned, and is it working?
<--- Score

94. What do you measure to verify effectiveness gains?
<--- Score

95. Are documented procedures clear and easy to follow for the operators?
<--- Score

96. Does the response plan contain a definite closed loop continual improvement scheme (e.g., plan-do-check-act)?
<--- Score

97. How do you plan for the cost of succession?
<--- Score

Add up total points for this section:
_ _ _ _ _  = Total points for this section

Divided by: _ _ _ _ _ _  (number of statements answered) =  _ _ _ _ _ _
Average score for this section

Transfer your score to the knowledge assets Index at the beginning of the Self-Assessment.

# CRITERION #7: SUSTAIN:

INTENT: Retain the benefits.

In my belief, the answer to this question is clearly defined:

5 Strongly Agree

4 Agree

3 Neutral

2 Disagree

1 Strongly Disagree

1. Do you have past knowledge assets successes?
<--- Score

2. Are you satisfied with your current role?  If not, what is missing from it?
<--- Score

3. What are internal and external knowledge assets relations?
<--- Score

4. Is it economical; do you have the time and money?
<--- Score

**5. What technologies are used to ensure secure access to knowledge assets?**
<--- Score

6. Who will provide the final approval of knowledge assets deliverables?
<--- Score

7. Are there any activities that you can take off your to do list?
<--- Score

8. Are you / should you be revolutionary or evolutionary?
<--- Score

9. To whom do you add value?
<--- Score

10. How do you lead with knowledge assets in mind?
<--- Score

11. What would you recommend your friend do if he/she were facing this dilemma?
<--- Score

12. Is there any existing knowledge assets governance structure?
<--- Score

13. How do you govern and fulfill your societal responsibilities?
<--- Score

14. Ask yourself: how would you do this work if you only had one staff member to do it?
<--- Score

15. Who is the main stakeholder, with ultimate responsibility for driving knowledge assets forward?
<--- Score

**16. In the normal course of business, who has access to your organizations knowledge assets?**
<--- Score

17. How do you proactively clarify deliverables and knowledge assets quality expectations?
<--- Score

18. How do you maintain knowledge assets's Integrity?
<--- Score

19. What was the last experiment you ran?
<--- Score

20. Who have you, as a company, historically been when you've been at your best?
<--- Score

21. What is an unauthorized commitment?
<--- Score

22. What is the estimated value of the project?
<--- Score

23. If you find that you havent accomplished one of the goals for one of the steps of the knowledge assets

strategy, what will you do to fix it?
<--- Score

24. Are you making progress, and are you making progress as knowledge assets leaders?
<--- Score

25. Who is responsible for knowledge assets?
<--- Score

26. Can you maintain your growth without detracting from the factors that have contributed to your success?
<--- Score

27. Who will manage the integration of tools?
<--- Score

28. What do we do when new problems arise?
<--- Score

29. Why should you adopt a knowledge assets framework?
<--- Score

30. If you got fired and a new hire took your place, what would she do different?
<--- Score

31. Who will be responsible for deciding whether knowledge assets goes ahead or not after the initial investigations?
<--- Score

32. What is the craziest thing you can do?
<--- Score

33. What unique value proposition (UVP) do you offer?
<--- Score

34. How do senior leaders deploy your organizations vision and values through your leadership system, to the workforce, to key suppliers and partners, and to customers and other stakeholders, as appropriate?
<--- Score

35. Have benefits been optimized with all key stakeholders?
<--- Score

36. What is your question? Why?
<--- Score

37. How do you listen to customers to obtain actionable information?
<--- Score

38. Instead of going to current contacts for new ideas, what if you reconnected with dormant contacts-- the people you used to know?  If you were going reactivate a dormant tie, who would it be?
<--- Score

39. How do you make it meaningful in connecting knowledge assets with what users do day-to-day?
<--- Score

40. Can you break it down?
<--- Score

41. Do you think you know, or do you know you know ?

<--- Score

42. How can you become the company that would put you out of business?
<--- Score

43. Do knowledge assets rules make a reasonable demand on a users capabilities?
<--- Score

**44. How valuable do you believe your trade secrets or knowledge assets are to an attacker?**
<--- Score

45. How do you know if you are successful?
<--- Score

46. Operational - will it work?
<--- Score

47. Do you feel that more should be done in the knowledge assets area?
<--- Score

48. In a project to restructure knowledge assets outcomes, which stakeholders would you involve?
<--- Score

49. How much contingency will be available in the budget?
<--- Score

50. Which knowledge assets goals are the most important?
<--- Score

51. How can you incorporate support to ensure safe and effective use of knowledge assets into the services that you provide?
<--- Score

52. How do you set knowledge assets stretch targets and how do you get people to not only participate in setting these stretch targets but also that they strive to achieve these?
<--- Score

53. Is a knowledge assets breakthrough on the horizon?
<--- Score

54. What one word do you want to own in the minds of your customers, employees, and partners?
<--- Score

55. Who is responsible for errors?
<--- Score

56. What is something you believe that nearly no one agrees with you on?
<--- Score

57. What are the challenges?
<--- Score

58. If you had to rebuild your organization without any traditional competitive advantages (i.e., no killer technology, promising research, innovative product/ service delivery model, etcetera), how would your people have to approach their work and collaborate together in order to create the necessary conditions for success?

<--- Score

59. Were lessons learned captured and communicated?
<--- Score

60. Do you think knowledge assets accomplishes the goals you expect it to accomplish?
<--- Score

61. What may be the consequences for the performance of an organization if all stakeholders are not consulted regarding knowledge assets?
<--- Score

62. Would you rather sell to knowledgeable and informed customers or to uninformed customers?
<--- Score

63. Whose voice (department, ethnic group, women, older workers, etc) might you have missed hearing from in your company, and how might you amplify this voice to create positive momentum for your business?
<--- Score

64. Who do you want your customers to become?
<--- Score

65. What is the recommended frequency of auditing?
<--- Score

66. What knowledge assets modifications can you make work for you?
<--- Score

67. How can you negotiate knowledge assets successfully with a stubborn boss, an irate client, or a deceitful coworker?
<--- Score

68. What role does communication play in the success or failure of a knowledge assets project?
<--- Score

69. Who do you think the world wants your organization to be?
<--- Score

70. What are the long-term knowledge assets goals?
<--- Score

71. Why is it important to have senior management support for a knowledge assets project?
<--- Score

72. How do you assess the knowledge assets pitfalls that are inherent in implementing it?
<--- Score

73. Who are your customers?
<--- Score

**74. What are the challenges in measuring your organizations knowledge assets?**
<--- Score

75. Why is knowledge assets important for you now?
<--- Score

76. If your customer were your grandmother, would you tell her to buy what you're selling?

<--- Score

77. Where can you break convention?
<--- Score

78. How do you create buy-in?
<--- Score

79. How do you manage knowledge assets
Knowledge Management (KM)?
<--- Score

80. What is the purpose of knowledge assets in
relation to the mission?
<--- Score

81. What are the short and long-term knowledge
assets goals?
<--- Score

82. What have been your experiences in defining long
range knowledge assets goals?
<--- Score

83. What goals did you miss?
<--- Score

84. What is the overall talent health of your
organization as a whole at senior levels, and for each
organization reporting to a member of the Senior
Leadership Team?
<--- Score

85. Who uses your product in ways you never
expected?
<--- Score

86. Why not do knowledge assets?
<--- Score

87. What management system can you use to leverage the knowledge assets experience, ideas, and concerns of the people closest to the work to be done?
<--- Score

88. What knowledge assets skills are most important?
<--- Score

89. What will be the consequences to the stakeholder (financial, reputation etc) if knowledge assets does not go ahead or fails to deliver the objectives?
<--- Score

90. What counts that you are not counting?
<--- Score

91. What is your competitive advantage?
<--- Score

92. What is effective knowledge assets?
<--- Score

93. Has implementation been effective in reaching specified objectives so far?
<--- Score

94. What are the business goals knowledge assets is aiming to achieve?
<--- Score

95. How will you ensure you get what you expected?

<--- Score

**96. Are you measuring your knowledge assets?**
<--- Score

97. What current systems have to be understood and/
or changed?
<--- Score

98. How do you cross-sell and up-sell your knowledge
assets success?
<--- Score

99. Can you do all this work?
<--- Score

100. How do you transition from the baseline to the
target?
<--- Score

101. How can you become more high-tech but still be
high touch?
<--- Score

102. Who are the key stakeholders?
<--- Score

103. Who else should you help?
<--- Score

104. What are the top 3 things at the forefront of your
knowledge assets agendas for the next 3 years?
<--- Score

105. How do you deal with knowledge assets
changes?

<--- Score

106. What projects are going on in the organization today, and what resources are those projects using from the resource pools?
<--- Score

107. How will you motivate the stakeholders with the least vested interest?
<--- Score

108. Who, on the executive team or the board, has spoken to a customer recently?
<--- Score

109. How do customers see your organization?
<--- Score

110. Marketing budgets are tighter, consumers are more skeptical, and social media has changed forever the way we talk about knowledge assets, how do you gain traction?
<--- Score

111. How do you foster innovation?
<--- Score

112. How are you doing compared to your industry?
<--- Score

113. What is the big knowledge assets idea?
<--- Score

114. How do you determine the key elements that affect knowledge assets workforce satisfaction, how are these elements determined for different workforce

groups and segments?
<--- Score

115. Think of your knowledge assets project, what are the main functions?
<--- Score

116. What happens if you do not have enough funding?
<--- Score

**117. Do third parties have access to your organizations knowledge assets?**
<--- Score

118. Are you paying enough attention to the partners your company depends on to succeed?
<--- Score

119. What have you done to protect your business from competitive encroachment?
<--- Score

120. What new services of functionality will be implemented next with knowledge assets ?
<--- Score

121. If you weren't already in this business, would you enter it today? And if not, what are you going to do about it?
<--- Score

122. What are the barriers to increased knowledge assets production?
<--- Score

123. Do you see more potential in people than they do in themselves?
<--- Score

124. How do you provide a safe environment -physically and emotionally?
<--- Score

125. Is there any reason to believe the opposite of my current belief?
<--- Score

126. Is your strategy driving your strategy? Or is the way in which you allocate resources driving your strategy?
<--- Score

127. How do you track customer value, profitability or financial return, organizational success, and sustainability?
<--- Score

128. What is the funding source for this project?
<--- Score

129. What happens at your organization when people fail?
<--- Score

130. What are the key enablers to make this knowledge assets move?
<--- Score

131. Who are four people whose careers you have enhanced?
<--- Score

132. Why do and why don't your customers like your organization?
<--- Score

133. How long will it take to change?
<--- Score

134. Do you have the right capabilities and capacities?
<--- Score

135. Is the knowledge assets organization completing tasks effectively and efficiently?
<--- Score

136. Which models, tools and techniques are necessary?
<--- Score

137. How likely is it that a customer would recommend your company to a friend or colleague?
<--- Score

138. What should you stop doing?
<--- Score

139. Is the impact that knowledge assets has shown?
<--- Score

140. What is your BATNA (best alternative to a negotiated agreement)?
<--- Score

141. If you do not follow, then how to lead?
<--- Score

142. Are you relevant? Will you be relevant five years from now? Ten?
<--- Score

143. What stupid rule would you most like to kill?
<--- Score

144. What is the kind of project structure that would be appropriate for your knowledge assets project, should it be formal and complex, or can it be less formal and relatively simple?
<--- Score

145. Who do we want your customers to become?
<--- Score

146. How do you keep records, of what?
<--- Score

147. Is there a work around that you can use?
<--- Score

148. If there were zero limitations, what would you do differently?
<--- Score

149. If you had to leave your organization for a year and the only communication you could have with employees/colleagues was a single paragraph, what would you write?
<--- Score

150. How does knowledge assets integrate with other stakeholder initiatives?
<--- Score

151. Is knowledge assets dependent on the successful delivery of a current project?
<--- Score

152. How do you ensure that implementations of knowledge assets products are done in a way that ensures safety?
<--- Score

153. What is your formula for success in knowledge assets ?
<--- Score

154. Who is responsible for ensuring appropriate resources (time, people and money) are allocated to knowledge assets?
<--- Score

155. Is a knowledge assets team work effort in place?
<--- Score

156. Are you maintaining a past–present–future perspective throughout the knowledge assets discussion?
<--- Score

157. Is your basic point _____ or _____?
<--- Score

158. What are you challenging?
<--- Score

159. Political -is anyone trying to undermine this project?
<--- Score

160. What is the source of the strategies for knowledge assets strengthening and reform?
<--- Score

161. What are you trying to prove to yourself, and how might it be hijacking your life and business success?
<--- Score

162. What is the overall business strategy?
<--- Score

163. What are your personal philosophies regarding knowledge assets and how do they influence your work?
<--- Score

164. What relationships among knowledge assets trends do you perceive?
<--- Score

165. Who is on the team?
<--- Score

166. Do you have an implicit bias for capital investments over people investments?
<--- Score

167. What is it like to work for you?
<--- Score

168. Are you changing as fast as the world around you?
<--- Score

169. What are current knowledge assets paradigms?
<--- Score

170. What are your most important goals for the strategic knowledge assets objectives?
<--- Score

171. What trophy do you want on your mantle?
<--- Score

172. Will there be any necessary staff changes (redundancies or new hires)?
<--- Score

173. How do you engage the workforce, in addition to satisfying them?
<--- Score

174. Do you know what you are doing? And who do you call if you don't?
<--- Score

175. Do you know who is a friend or a foe?
<--- Score

176. What are the usability implications of knowledge assets actions?
<--- Score

177. What is the range of capabilities?
<--- Score

178. What are the gaps in your knowledge and experience?
<--- Score

179. How will you know that the knowledge assets project has been successful?

<--- Score

180. What you are going to do to affect the numbers?
<--- Score

**181. Does your organization have a program or set of activities for managing knowledge assets?**
<--- Score

182. What are the essentials of internal knowledge assets management?
<--- Score

183. What are the potential basics of knowledge assets fraud?
<--- Score

**184. What are the key areas of knowledge, and what are your key knowledge assets that, if you managed them better, would make a big difference to achieving your organizations objectives?**
<--- Score

185. What trouble can you get into?
<--- Score

**186. Do you have any involvement in managing knowledge assets?**
<--- Score

187. How much does knowledge assets help?
<--- Score

188. If no one would ever find out about your accomplishments, how would you lead differently?

<--- Score

189. What did you miss in the interview for the worst hire you ever made?
<--- Score

190. What business benefits will knowledge assets goals deliver if achieved?
<--- Score

191. Do you have the right people on the bus?
<--- Score

192. If you were responsible for initiating and implementing major changes in your organization, what steps might you take to ensure acceptance of those changes?
<--- Score

193. Can the schedule be done in the given time?
<--- Score

194. What is a feasible sequencing of reform initiatives over time?
<--- Score

195. Are you using a design thinking approach and integrating Innovation, knowledge assets Experience, and Brand Value?
<--- Score

196. What would have to be true for the option on the table to be the best possible choice?
<--- Score

197. What knowledge, skills and characteristics mark a

good knowledge assets project manager?
<--- Score

198. Why will customers want to buy your organizations products/services?
<--- Score

199. Whom among your colleagues do you trust, and for what?
<--- Score

200. How do you stay inspired?
<--- Score

201. What could happen if you do not do it?
<--- Score

202. Do you say no to customers for no reason?
<--- Score

**203. How familiar are you with your organizations approach to managing knowledge assets?**
<--- Score

204. Are your responses positive or negative?
<--- Score

205. What potential megatrends could make your business model obsolete?
<--- Score

206. What must you excel at?
<--- Score

207. Are the criteria for selecting recommendations stated?

<--- Score

208. Which functions and people interact with the supplier and or customer?
<--- Score

209. How important is knowledge assets to the user organizations mission?
<--- Score

210. Are all key stakeholders present at all Structured Walkthroughs?
<--- Score

211. Do you have enough freaky customers in your portfolio pushing you to the limit day in and day out?
<--- Score

212. What information is critical to your organization that your executives are ignoring?
<--- Score

213. What threat is knowledge assets addressing?
<--- Score

214. What are the rules and assumptions your industry operates under? What if the opposite were true?
<--- Score

215. Why should people listen to you?
<--- Score

216. How do you foster the skills, knowledge, talents, attributes, and characteristics you want to have?
<--- Score

217. Are new benefits received and understood?
<--- Score

218. Which individuals, teams or departments will be involved in knowledge assets?
<--- Score

219. Who will determine interim and final deadlines?
<--- Score

220. How do you go about securing knowledge assets?
<--- Score

221. Are the assumptions believable and achievable?
<--- Score

222. Is maximizing knowledge assets protection the same as minimizing knowledge assets loss?
<--- Score

223. How will you insure seamless interoperability of knowledge assets moving forward?
<--- Score

224. Have new benefits been realized?
<--- Score

225. Are assumptions made in knowledge assets stated explicitly?
<--- Score

226. At what moment would you think; Will I get fired?
<--- Score

227. How is implementation research currently

incorporated into each of your goals?
<--- Score

228. What happens when a new employee joins the organization?
<--- Score

229. How do you accomplish your long range knowledge assets goals?
<--- Score

230. What are specific knowledge assets rules to follow?
<--- Score

231. In retrospect, of the projects that you pulled the plug on, what percent do you wish had been allowed to keep going, and what percent do you wish had ended earlier?
<--- Score

232. What is your knowledge assets strategy?
<--- Score

233. What are strategies for increasing support and reducing opposition?
<--- Score

234. In the past year, what have you done (or could you have done) to increase the accurate perception of your company/brand as ethical and honest?
<--- Score

235. When information truly is ubiquitous, when reach and connectivity are completely global, when computing resources are infinite, and when a whole

new set of impossibilities are not only possible, but happening, what will that do to your business?
<--- Score

236. How do you keep the momentum going?
<--- Score

237. Is knowledge assets realistic, or are you setting yourself up for failure?
<--- Score

238. Will it be accepted by users?
<--- Score

239. Did your employees make progress today?
<--- Score

240. If your company went out of business tomorrow, would anyone who doesn't get a paycheck here care?
<--- Score

241. What are the success criteria that will indicate that knowledge assets objectives have been met and the benefits delivered?
<--- Score

242. What does your signature ensure?
<--- Score

**243. What technologies are used to secure access to knowledge assets?**
<--- Score

Add up total points for this section:
_ _ _ _ _  = Total points for this section

Divided by: _____ (number of
statements answered) = _____
Average score for this section

Transfer your score to the knowledge
assets Index at the beginning of the
Self-Assessment.

# knowledge assets and Managing Projects, Criteria for Project Managers:

# 1.0 Initiating Process Group: knowledge assets

1. Were resources available as planned?

2. How is each deliverable reviewed, verified, and validated?

3. What must be done?

4. Were decisions made in a timely manner?

5. Did the knowledge assets project team have the right skills?

6. What are the constraints?

7. Do you know the knowledge assets projects goal, purpose and objectives?

8. Who is funding the knowledge assets project?

9. Do you know all the stakeholders impacted by the knowledge assets project and what needs are?

10. What technical work to do in each phase?

11. Does the knowledge assets project team have enough people to execute the knowledge assets project plan?

12. What are the overarching issues of your organization?

13. Did the knowledge assets project team have the

right skills?

14. Do you understand all business (operational), technical, resource and vendor risks associated with the knowledge assets project?

15. Are stakeholders properly informed about the status of the knowledge assets project?

16. How do you help others satisfy needs?

17. Were escalated issues resolved promptly?

18. Have you evaluated the teams performance and asked for feedback?

19. How well defined and documented were the knowledge assets project management processes you chose to use?

20. The knowledge assets project you are managing has nine stakeholders. How many channel of communications are there between corresponding stakeholders?

# 1.1 Project Charter: knowledge assets

21. Strategic fit: what is the strategic initiative identifier for this knowledge assets project?

22. Avoid costs, improve service, and/ or comply with a mandate?

23. What goes into your knowledge assets project Charter?

24. What are the deliverables?

25. Fit with other Products Compliments – Cannibalizes?

26. What is the justification?

27. Why have you chosen the aim you have set forth?

28. How do you manage integration?

29. What are the known stakeholder requirements?

30. What are you trying to accomplish?

31. How will you know that a change is an improvement?

32. What are some examples of a business case?

33. Why use a knowledge assets project charter?

34. What are the assumptions?

35. Are there special technology requirements?

36. Is it an improvement over existing products?

37. What does it need to do?

38. Did your knowledge assets project ask for this?

39. Market – identify products market, including whether it is outside of the objective: what is the purpose of the program or knowledge assets project?

40. Customer benefits: what customer requirements does this knowledge assets project address?

## 1.2 Stakeholder Register: knowledge assets

41. What is the power of the stakeholder?

42. Is your organization ready for change?

43. How will reports be created?

44. How big is the gap?

45. What opportunities exist to provide communications?

46. How much influence do they have on the knowledge assets project?

47. Who is managing stakeholder engagement?

48. Who are the stakeholders?

49. What & Why?

50. What are the major knowledge assets project milestones requiring communications or providing communications opportunities?

51. Who wants to talk about Security?

52. How should employers make voices heard?

# 1.3 Stakeholder Analysis Matrix: knowledge assets

53. Who will be affected by the work?

54. What is the relationship among stakeholders?

55. What are the opportunities for communication?

56. Guiding question: who shall you involve in the making of the stakeholder map?

57. Are there people who ise voices or interests in the issue may not be heard?

58. What is your organizations competitors doing?

59. What do people from other organizations see as your organizations weaknesses?

60. Are you going to weigh the stakeholders?

61. Sustaining internal capabilities?

62. How to measure the achievement of the Outputs?

63. Inoculations or payment to receive them?

64. Who holds positions of responsibility in interested organizations?

65. Where are mitigation costs factored in?

66. Opponents; who are the opponents?

67. Global influences?

68. Who has control over whom?

69. What do you Evaluate?

70. Location and geographical?

71. What is the stakeholders mandate, what is mission?

# 2.0 Planning Process Group: knowledge assets

72. What is the critical path for this knowledge assets project, and what is the duration of the critical path?

73. How well do the team follow the chosen processes?

74. How can you make your needs known?

75. Explanation: is what the knowledge assets project intents to solve a hard question?

76. Are you just doing busywork to pass the time?

77. What should you do next?

78. How will you do it?

79. What do you need to do?

80. Are work methodologies, financial instruments, etc. shared among departments, organizations and knowledge assets projects?

81. How should needs be met?

82. If task x starts two days late, what is the effect on the knowledge assets project end date?

83. To what extent have the target population and participants made the activities own, taking an active

role in it?

84. In what ways can the governance of the knowledge assets project be improved so that it has greater likelihood of achieving future sustainability?

85. In what way has the knowledge assets project come up with innovative measures for problem-solving?

86. How will it affect you?

87. On which process should team members spend the most time?

88. Professionals want to know what is expected from them; what are the deliverables?

89. Will the products created live up to the necessary quality?

90. Why do it knowledge assets projects fail?

91. To what extent are the participating departments coordinating with each other?

## 2.1 Project Management Plan: knowledge assets

92. Are alternatives safe, functional, constructible, economical, reasonable and sustainable?

93. What are the assigned resources?

94. Are there any Client staffing expectations?

95. When is a knowledge assets project management plan created?

96. What goes into your knowledge assets project Charter?

97. How well are you able to manage your risk?

98. Does the selected plan protect privacy?

99. How do you manage time?

100. Are there any windfall benefits that would accrue to the knowledge assets project sponsor or other parties?

101. Are calculations and results of analyzes essentially correct?

102. What should you drop in order to add something new?

103. What would you do differently what did not

work?

104. How do you organize the costs in the knowledge assets project management plan?

105. Is there an incremental analysis/cost effectiveness analysis of proposed mitigation features based on an approved method and using an accepted model?

106. Is mitigation authorized or recommended?

107. If the knowledge assets project management plan is a comprehensive document that guides you in knowledge assets project execution and control, then what should it NOT contain?

108. Are the proposed knowledge assets project purposes different than a previously authorized knowledge assets project?

109. What would you do differently?

## 2.2 Scope Management Plan: knowledge assets

110. Does all knowledge assets project documentation reside in a common repository for easy access?

111. Pareto diagrams, statistical sampling, flow charting or trend analysis used quality monitoring?

112. Are the people assigned to the knowledge assets project sufficiently qualified?

113. What are the Quality Assurance overheads?

114. Is the communication plan being followed?

115. Do all stakeholders know how to access this repository and where to find the knowledge assets project documentation?

116. What went right?

117. Do you secure formal approval of changes and requirements from stakeholders?

118. Have all team members been part of identifying risks?

119. What went wrong?

120. What are the risks that could significantly affect the scope of the knowledge assets project?

121. Are schedule deliverables actually delivered?

122. Are the payment terms being followed?

123. What work performance data will be captured?

124. To whom will the deliverables be first presented for inspection and verification?

125. Sensitivity analysis?

126. What are the risks of not having good inter-organization cooperation on the knowledge assets project?

127. Are risk oriented checklists used during risk identification?

128. What are the risks that could significantly affect procuring consultant staff for the knowledge assets project?

129. Where do scope management processes fit in?

## 2.3 Requirements Management Plan: knowledge assets

130. Who is responsible for monitoring and tracking the knowledge assets project requirements?

131. Do you understand the role that each stakeholder will play in the requirements process?

132. Is the system software (non-operating system) new to the IT knowledge assets project team?

133. Will you use an assessment of the knowledge assets project environment as a tool to discover risk to the requirements process?

134. Is any organizational data being used or stored?

135. Is stakeholder risk tolerance an important factor for the requirements process in this knowledge assets project?

136. Why manage requirements?

137. How will unresolved questions be handled once approval has been obtained?

138. Who will do the reporting and to whom will reports be delivered?

139. Has the requirements team been instructed in the Change Control process?

140. How often will the reporting occur?

141. What performance metrics will be used?

142. Who will finally present the work or product(s) for acceptance?

143. Did you get proper approvals?

144. What is the earliest finish date for this knowledge assets project if it is scheduled to start on ...?

145. Do you really need to write this document at all?

146. How will requirements be managed?

147. Did you provide clear and concise specifications?

148. Will you perform a Requirements Risk assessment and develop a plan to deal with risks?

## 2.4 Requirements Documentation: knowledge assets

149. Are there legal issues?

150. Have the benefits identified with the system being identified clearly?

151. Who provides requirements?

152. Are there any requirements conflicts?

153. What are the potential disadvantages/ advantages?

154. How can you document system requirements?

155. Do technical resources exist?

156. What can tools do for us?

157. Who is interacting with the system?

158. Where do you define what is a customer, what are the attributes of customer?

159. Verifiability. can the requirements be checked?

160. Is the origin of the requirement clearly stated?

161. How do you get the user to tell you what they want?

162. Where are business rules being captured?

163. Can the requirements be checked?

164. Validity. does the system provide the functions which best support the customers needs?

165. Are all functions required by the customer included?

166. What is effective documentation?

167. Consistency. are there any requirements conflicts?

168. How does the proposed knowledge assets project contribute to the overall objectives of your organization?

## 2.5 Requirements Traceability Matrix: knowledge assets

169. Describe the process for approving requirements so they can be added to the traceability matrix and knowledge assets project work can be performed. Will the knowledge assets project requirements become approved in writing?

170. How do you manage scope?

171. Will you use a Requirements Traceability Matrix?

172. What percentage of knowledge assets projects are producing traceability matrices between requirements and other work products?

173. How will it affect the stakeholders personally in career?

174. Why use a WBS?

175. What is the WBS?

176. What are the chronologies, contingencies, consequences, criteria?

177. Is there a requirements traceability process in place?

178. How small is small enough?

179. Do you have a clear understanding of all

subcontracts in place?

180. Why do you manage scope?

## 2.6 Project Scope Statement: knowledge assets

181. Has everyone approved the knowledge assets projects scope statement?

182. Has a method and process for requirement tracking been developed?

183. Will all tasks resulting from issues be entered into the knowledge assets project Plan and tracked through the plan?

184. knowledge assets project lead, team lead, solution architect?

185. If there is an independent oversight contractor, have they signed off on the knowledge assets project Plan?

186. Is the scope of your knowledge assets project well defined?

187. Elements of scope management that deal with concept development ?

188. Do you anticipate new stakeholders joining the knowledge assets project over time?

189. Has the knowledge assets project scope statement been reviewed as part of the baseline process?

190. What is the product of this knowledge assets project?

191. Will the knowledge assets project risks be managed according to the knowledge assets projects risk management process?

192. Was planning completed before the knowledge assets project was initiated?

193. Were potential customers involved early in the planning process?

194. What is a process you might recommend to verify the accuracy of the research deliverable?

195. Will the risk plan be updated on a regular and frequent basis?

196. Elements that deal with providing the detail?

197. Any new risks introduced or old risks impacted. Are there issues that could affect the existing requirements for the result, service, or product if the scope changes?

198. Are there issues that could affect the existing requirements for the result, service, or product if the scope changes?

199. Which risks does the knowledge assets project focus on?

200. Is there a Quality Assurance Plan documented and filed?

## 2.7 Assumption and Constraint Log: knowledge assets

201. Is there adequate stakeholder participation for the vetting of requirements definition, changes and management?

202. If it is out of compliance, should the process be amended or should the Plan be amended?

203. Does the system design reflect the requirements?

204. Do the requirements meet the standards of correctness, completeness, consistency, accuracy, and readability?

205. What do you audit?

206. Can you perform this task or activity in a more effective manner?

207. Would known impacts serve as impediments?

208. Does a specific action and/or state that is known to violate security policy occur?

209. Are there processes defining how software will be developed including development methods, overall timeline for development, software product standards, and traceability?

210. Diagrams and tables are included to account for complex concepts and increase overall readability?

211. What strengths do you have?

212. Is this process still needed?

213. Are requirements management tracking tools and procedures in place?

214. Is the current scope of the knowledge assets project substantially different than that originally defined in the approved knowledge assets project plan?

215. Should factors be unpredictable over time?

216. Security analysis has access to information that is sanitized?

217. How do you design an auditing system?

218. Are you meeting your customers expectations consistently?

219. How can constraints be violated?

220. Are there nonconformance issues?

## 2.8 Work Breakdown Structure: knowledge assets

221. What has to be done?

222. Is the work breakdown structure (wbs) defined and is the scope of the knowledge assets project clear with assigned deliverable owners?

223. When do you stop?

224. What is the probability of completing the knowledge assets project in less that xx days?

225. How many levels?

226. Do you need another level?

227. What is the probability that the knowledge assets project duration will exceed xx weeks?

228. Is it still viable?

229. How big is a work-package?

230. Why would you develop a Work Breakdown Structure?

231. How far down?

232. Who has to do it?

233. When does it have to be done?

234. How will you and your knowledge assets project team define the knowledge assets projects scope and work breakdown structure?

235. How much detail?

236. Is it a change in scope?

237. Where does it take place?

238. Why is it useful?

# 2.9 WBS Dictionary: knowledge assets

239. Are estimates of costs at completion generated in a rational, consistent manner?

240. Does the sum of all work package budgets plus planning packages within control accounts equal the budgets assigned to the already stated control accounts?

241. Does the scheduling system identify in a timely manner the status of work?

242. Are the variances between budgeted and actual indirect costs identified and analyzed at the level of assigned responsibility for control (indirect pool, department, etc.)?

243. Should you have a test for each code module?

244. Does the contractors system provide for the determination of cost variances attributable to the excess usage of material?

245. Budgeted cost for work performed?

246. Changes in the overhead pool and/or organization structures?

247. Detailed schedules which support control account and work package start and completion dates/events?

248. Are the overhead pools formally and adequately

identified?

249. Are the procedures for identifying indirect costs to incurring organizations, indirect cost pools, and allocating the costs from the pools to the contracts formally documented?

250. Incurrence of actual indirect costs in excess of budgets, by element of expense?

251. Are knowledge assets projected overhead costs in each pool and the associated direct costs used as the basis for establishing interim rates for allocating overhead to contracts?

252. Are internal budgets for authorized, and not priced changes based on the contractors resource plan for accomplishing the work?

253. Is authorization of budgets in excess of the contract budget base controlled formally and done with the full knowledge and recognition of the procuring activity?

254. Changes in the nature of the overhead requirements?

255. Is each control account assigned to a single organizational element directly responsible for the work and identifiable to a single element of the CWBS?

256. Authorization to proceed with all authorized work?

# 2.10 Schedule Management Plan: knowledge assets

257. Is the development plan and/or process documented?

258. Are meeting objectives identified for each meeting?

259. Are post milestone knowledge assets project reviews (PMPR) conducted with your organization at least once a year?

260. Are metrics used to evaluate and manage Vendors?

261. What threats might prevent you from getting there?

262. Have reserves been created to address risks?

263. Have the procedures for identifying budget variances been followed?

264. Are the people assigned to the knowledge assets project sufficiently qualified?

265. How does the proposed individual meet each requirement?

266. Are all payments made according to the contract(s)?

267. Are action items captured and managed?

268. Has a sponsor been identified?

269. Are there any activities or deliverables being added or gold-plated that could be dropped or scaled back without falling short of the original requirement?

270. Identify the amount of schedule variation that triggers a warning. What happens if a warning is triggered?

271. Do knowledge assets project teams & team members report on status / activities / progress?

272. Does the schedule have reasonable float?

273. Are trade-offs between accepting the risk and mitigating the risk identified?

274. Are knowledge assets project contact logs kept up to date?

275. Staffing Requirements?

# 2.11 Activity List: knowledge assets

276. Where will it be performed?

277. What is the probability the knowledge assets project can be completed in xx weeks?

278. Are the required resources available or need to be acquired?

279. Is infrastructure setup part of your knowledge assets project?

280. How difficult will it be to do specific activities on this knowledge assets project?

281. Can you determine the activity that must finish, before this activity can start?

282. How can the knowledge assets project be displayed graphically to better visualize the activities?

283. What is your organizations history in doing similar activities?

284. When will the work be performed?

285. Should you include sub-activities?

286. How will it be performed?

287. How detailed should a knowledge assets project get?

288. In what sequence?

289. What is the LF and LS for each activity?

290. What will be performed?

291. What are you counting on?

292. What went well?

293. Is there anything planned that does not need to be here?

294. For other activities, how much delay can be tolerated?

295. When do the individual activities need to start and finish?

# 2.12 Activity Attributes: knowledge assets

296. Resource is assigned to?

297. How many resources do you need to complete the work scope within a limit of X number of days?

298. Activity: what is Missing?

299. Do you feel very comfortable with your prediction?

300. Can more resources be added?

301. Does your organization of the data change its meaning?

302. Would you consider either of corresponding activities an outlier?

303. Which method produces the more accurate cost assignment?

304. Activity: what is In the Bag?

305. What activity do you think you should spend the most time on?

306. Activity: fair or not fair?

307. What conclusions/generalizations can you draw from this?

308. Where else does it apply?

309. How difficult will it be to do specific activities on this knowledge assets project?

310. Is there a trend during the year?

311. Time for overtime?

312. How else could the items be grouped?

# 2.13 Milestone List: knowledge assets

313. How soon can the activity start?

314. How will the milestone be verified?

315. What would happen if a delivery of material was one week late?

316. How late can each activity be finished and started?

317. Competitive advantages?

318. Information and research?

319. Describe your organizations strengths and core competencies. What factors will make your organization succeed?

320. New USPs?

321. Own known vulnerabilities?

322. What is the market for your technology, product or service?

323. How difficult will it be to do specific activities on this knowledge assets project?

324. What has been done so far?

325. What specific improvements did you make to the knowledge assets project proposal since the previous

time?

326. Describe the concept of the technology, product or service that will be or has been developed. How will it be used?

327. Marketing - reach, distribution, awareness?

328. What background experience, skills, and strengths does the team bring to your organization?

329. Loss of key staff?

330. How soon can the activity finish?

331. Insurmountable weaknesses?

# 2.14 Network Diagram: knowledge assets

332. If x is long, what would be the completion time if you break x into two parallel parts of y weeks and z weeks?

333. What job or jobs precede it?

334. How difficult will it be to do specific activities on this knowledge assets project?

335. What are the Key Success Factors?

336. Review the logical flow of the network diagram. Take a look at which activities you have first and then sequence the activities. Do they make sense?

337. Why must you schedule milestones, such as reviews, throughout the knowledge assets project?

338. Are you on time?

339. What must be completed before an activity can be started?

340. What is the probability of completing the knowledge assets project in less that xx days?

341. Which type of network diagram allows you to depict four types of dependencies?

342. Are the required resources available?

343. What is the lowest cost to complete this knowledge assets project in xx weeks?

344. If a current contract exists, can you provide the vendor name, contract start, and contract expiration date?

345. What job or jobs follow it?

346. How confident can you be in your milestone dates and the delivery date?

347. What controls the start and finish of a job?

348. What job or jobs could run concurrently?

349. Where do schedules come from?

## 2.15 Activity Resource Requirements: knowledge assets

350. Anything else?

351. What are constraints that you might find during the Human Resource Planning process?

352. How do you handle petty cash?

353. Why do you do that?

354. How many signatures do you require on a check and does this match what is in your policy and procedures?

355. Organizational Applicability?

356. Other support in specific areas?

357. Do you use tools like decomposition and rolling-wave planning to produce the activity list and other outputs?

358. Which logical relationship does the PDM use most often?

359. When does monitoring begin?

360. What is the Work Plan Standard?

361. Are there unresolved issues that need to be addressed?

## 2.16 Resource Breakdown Structure: knowledge assets

362. Which resource planning tool provides information on resource responsibility and accountability?

363. Any changes from stakeholders?

364. The list could probably go on, but, the thing that you would most like to know is, How long & How much?

365. Why time management?

366. What defines a successful knowledge assets project?

367. Changes based on input from stakeholders?

368. When do they need the information?

369. How difficult will it be to do specific activities on this knowledge assets project?

370. How can this help you with team building?

371. Which resources should be in the resource pool?

372. Is predictive resource analysis being done?

373. How should the information be delivered?

374. Goals for the knowledge assets project. What is each stakeholders desired outcome for the knowledge assets project?

375. Who will be used as a knowledge assets project team member?

376. Why do you do it?

## 2.17 Activity Duration Estimates: knowledge assets

377. What steps did your organization take to earn this prestigious quality award?

378. How difficult will it be to complete specific activities on this knowledge assets project?

379. What are the main types of contracts if you do decide to outsource?

380. Briefly describe some key events in the history of knowledge assets project management. What knowledge assets project was the first to use modern knowledge assets project management?

381. What is the critical path for this knowledge assets project and how long is it?

382. What distinguishes one organization from another in this area?

383. How do functionality, system outputs, performance, reliability, and maintainability requirements affect quality planning?

384. How have experts such as Deming, Juran, Crosby, and Taguchi affected the quality movement and todays use of Six Sigma?

385. How much time is required to develop it?

386. Research risk management software. Are many products available?

387. Will it help promote wellness at your organization and reduce insurance costs?

388. Are adjustments implemented to correct or prevent defects?

389. Could it have been avoided?

390. What is the shortest possible time it will take to complete this knowledge assets project?

391. Based on , if you need to shorten the duration of the knowledge assets project, what activity would you try to shorten?

392. Are procedures documented for managing risks?

393. How does the job market and current state of the economy affect human resource management?

394. Why do you think schedule issues often cause the most conflicts on knowledge assets projects?

395. What are the nine areas of expertise?

396. How many different communications channels does a knowledge assets project team with six people have?

## 2.18 Duration Estimating Worksheet: knowledge assets

397. How should ongoing costs be monitored to try to keep the knowledge assets project within budget?

398. When, then?

399. Science = process: remember the scientific method?

400. Done before proceeding with this activity or what can be done concurrently?

401. Is a construction detail attached (to aid in explanation)?

402. How can the knowledge assets project be displayed graphically to better visualize the activities?

403. What is the total time required to complete the knowledge assets project if no delays occur?

404. What is an Average knowledge assets project?

405. What work will be included in the knowledge assets project?

406. When does your organization expect to be able to complete it?

407. Why estimate time and cost?

408. Do any colleagues have experience with your organization and/or RFPs?

409. Will the knowledge assets project collaborate with the local community and leverage resources?

410. Define the work as completely as possible. What work will be included in the knowledge assets project?

411. Is the knowledge assets project responsive to community need?

412. What utility impacts are there?

## 2.19 Project Schedule: knowledge assets

413. Why or why not?

414. Have all knowledge assets project delays been adequately accounted for, communicated to all stakeholders and adjustments made in overall knowledge assets project schedule?

415. Why do you need schedules?

416. Verify that the update is accurate. Are all remaining durations correct?

417. Is knowledge assets project work proceeding in accordance with the original knowledge assets project schedule?

418. Are there activities that came from a template or previous knowledge assets project that are not applicable on this phase of this knowledge assets project?

419. Why do you think schedule issues often cause the most conflicts on knowledge assets projects?

420. Did the knowledge assets project come in under budget?

421. The wbs is developed as part of a joint planning session. and how do you know that youhave done this right?

422. Is the knowledge assets project schedule available for all knowledge assets project team members to review?

423. Are you working on the right risks?

424. How can you shorten the schedule?

425. How does a knowledge assets project get to be a year late ?

426. What is knowledge assets project management?

427. What is the difference?

428. How can you fix it?

429. knowledge assets project work estimates Who is managing the work estimate quality of work tasks in the knowledge assets project schedule?

## 2.20 Cost Management Plan: knowledge assets

430. Are adequate resources provided for the quality assurance function?

431. Has the schedule been baselined?

432. What is knowledge assets project cost management?

433. Are enough systems & user personnel assigned to the knowledge assets project?

434. Have all documents been archived in a knowledge assets project repository for each release?

435. Does the business case include how the knowledge assets project aligns with your organizations strategic goals & objectives?

436. Are target dates established for each milestone deliverable?

437. Is a stakeholder management plan in place that covers topics?

438. Progress measurement and control – How will the knowledge assets project measure and control progress?

439. Have knowledge assets project team accountabilities & responsibilities been clearly

defined?

440. Are key risk mitigation strategies added to the knowledge assets project schedule?

441. Exclusions – is there scope to be performed or provided by others?

442. Are the results of quality assurance reviews provided to affected groups & individuals?

443. Is the schedule updated on a periodic basis?

444. What weaknesses do you have?

445. Are corrective actions and variances reported?

446. Has the scope management document been updated and distributed to help prevent scope creep?

## 2.21 Activity Cost Estimates: knowledge assets

447. How do you treat administrative costs in the activity inventory?

448. Is costing method consistent with study goals?

449. Does the activity use a common approach or business function to deliver its results?

450. What is a knowledge assets project Management Plan?

451. Will you need to provide essential services information about activities?

452. Was it performed on time?

453. What were things that you need to improve?

454. Were the costs or charges reasonable?

455. The impact and what actions were taken?

456. Was the consultant knowledgeable about the program?

457. Is there anything unique in this knowledge assets projects scope statement that will affect resources?

458. What makes a good activity description?

459. How do you change activities?

460. Can you delete activities or make them inactive?

461. Who determines when the contractor is paid?

462. Did the knowledge assets project team have the right skills?

463. Does the activity rely on a common set of tools to carry it out?

464. Does the estimator have experience?

## 2.22 Cost Estimating Worksheet: knowledge assets

465. Who is best positioned to know and assist in identifying corresponding factors?

466. Ask: are others positioned to know, are others credible, and will others cooperate?

467. How will the results be shared and to whom?

468. Can a trend be established from historical performance data on the selected measure and are the criteria for using trend analysis or forecasting methods met?

469. Identify the timeframe necessary to monitor progress and collect data to determine how the selected measure has changed?

470. Value pocket identification & quantification what are value pockets?

471. What can be included?

472. What info is needed?

473. What is the purpose of estimating?

474. What costs are to be estimated?

475. Does the knowledge assets project provide innovative ways for stakeholders to overcome

obstacles or deliver better outcomes?

476. What additional knowledge assets project(s) could be initiated as a result of this knowledge assets project?

477. Is the knowledge assets project responsive to community need?

478. What happens to any remaining funds not used?

479. What is the estimated labor cost today based upon this information?

480. What will others want?

481. Is it feasible to establish a control group arrangement?

482. Will the knowledge assets project collaborate with the local community and leverage resources?

# 2.23 Cost Baseline: knowledge assets

483. What deliverables come first?

484. Will the knowledge assets project fail if the change request is not executed?

485. What is the most important thing to do next to make your knowledge assets project successful?

486. Are procedures defined by which the cost baseline may be changed?

487. Is the cr within knowledge assets project scope?

488. How likely is it to go wrong?

489. Definition of done can be traced back to the definitions of what are you providing to the customer in terms of deliverables?

490. Has training and knowledge transfer of the operations organization been completed?

491. What can go wrong?

492. Is there anything unique in this knowledge assets projects scope statement that will affect resources?

493. How fast?

494. How long are you willing to wait before you find out were late?

495. Impact to environment?

496. Has operations management formally accepted responsibility for operating and maintaining the product(s) or service(s) delivered by the knowledge assets project?

497. Have all approved changes to the knowledge assets project requirement been identified and impact on the performance, cost, and schedule baselines documented?

498. What do you want to measure ?

499. Are you asking management for something as a result of this update?

500. Why do you manage cost?

501. Has the appropriate access to relevant data and analysis capability been granted?

## 2.24 Quality Management Plan: knowledge assets

502. How does your organization establish and maintain customer relationships?

503. How is staff trained in procedures?

504. What changes can you make that will result in improvement?

505. Is there a Steering Committee in place?

506. Account for the procedures used to verify the data quality of the data being reviewed?

507. Diagrams and tables to account for complex concepts and increase overall readability?

508. How do senior leaders create your organizational focus on customers and other stakeholders?

509. Were the right locations/samples tested for the right parameters?

510. Contradictory information between different documents?

511. Does a documented knowledge assets project organizational policy & plan (i.e. governance model) exist?

512. What are the appropriate test methods to be

used?

513. How does your organization maintain a safe and healthy work environment?

514. How do you decide what information to record?

515. Are you following the quality standards?

516. How does your organization design processes to ensure others meet customer and others requirements?

517. How do your action plans support the strategic objectives?

518. Have adequate resources been provided by management to ensure knowledge assets project success?

519. Who gets results of work?

520. With the five whys method, the team considers why the issue being explored occurred. do others then take that initial answer and ask why?

## 2.25 Quality Metrics: knowledge assets

521. What can manufacturing professionals do to ensure quality is seen as an integral part of the entire product lifecycle?

522. When is the security analysis testing complete?

523. What metrics do you measure?

524. Which data do others need in one place to target areas of improvement?

525. Are quality metrics defined?

526. How does one achieve stability?

527. Is material complete (and does it meet the standards)?

528. Has trace of defects been initiated?

529. Can visual measures help you to filter visualizations of interest?

530. Can you correlate your quality metrics to profitability?

531. Do the operators focus on determining; is there anything you need to worry about?

532. What documentation is required?

533. What is the timeline to meet your goal?

534. Was the overall quality better or worse than previous products?

535. Has risk analysis been adequately reviewed?

536. Does risk analysis documentation meet standards?

537. How effective are your security tests?

538. Which report did you use to create the data you are submitting?

# 2.26 Process Improvement Plan: knowledge assets

539. How do you measure?

540. Are you meeting the quality standards?

541. Are you making progress on the improvement framework?

542. Are you making progress on the goals?

543. Has a process guide to collect the data been developed?

544. Does your process ensure quality?

545. Does explicit definition of the measures exist?

546. What actions are needed to address the problems and achieve the goals?

547. Are there forms and procedures to collect and record the data?

548. Where do you want to be?

549. What personnel are the change agents for your initiative?

550. What lessons have you learned so far?

551. If a process improvement framework is being

used, which elements will help the problems and goals listed?

552. Who should prepare the process improvement action plan?

553. Are you making progress on your improvement plan?

554. Modeling current processes is great, and will you ever see a return on that investment?

555. Has the time line required to move measurement results from the points of collection to databases or users been established?

556. What is the return on investment?

557. Where do you focus?

## 2.27 Responsibility Assignment Matrix: knowledge assets

558. Actual cost of work performed?

559. Is the entire contract planned in time-phased control accounts to the extent practicable?

560. Are meaningful indicators identified for use in measuring the status of cost and schedule performance?

561. Is work properly classified as measured effort, LOE, or apportioned effort and appropriately separated?

562. Are work packages assigned to performing organizations?

563. What is the number one predictor of a groups productivity?

564. Are people encouraged to bring up issues?

565. Changes in the current direct and knowledge assets projected base?

566. The already stated responsible for overhead performance control of related costs?

567. Performance to date and material commitment?

568. Contemplated overhead expenditure for each

period based on the best information currently available?

569. Are there any drawbacks to using a responsibility assignment matrix?

570. Do managers and team members provide helpful suggestions during review meetings?

571. Can the contractor substantiate work package and planning package budgets?

572. Does each role with Accountable responsibility have the authority within your organization to make the required decisions?

573. Do work packages consist of discrete tasks which are adequately described?

## 2.28 Roles and Responsibilities: knowledge assets

574. Who: who is involved?

575. What expectations were NOT met?

576. What is working well within your organizations performance management system?

577. Are knowledge assets project team roles and responsibilities identified and documented?

578. Was the expectation clearly communicated?

579. Who is responsible for implementation activities and where will the functions, roles and responsibilities be defined?

580. Is the data complete?

581. Is feedback clearly communicated and non-judgmental?

582. What specific behaviors did you observe?

583. Do you take the time to clearly define roles and responsibilities on knowledge assets project tasks?

584. Authority: what areas/knowledge assets projects in your work do you have the authority to decide upon and act on the already stated decisions?

585. What expectations were met?

586. Once the responsibilities are defined for the knowledge assets project, have the deliverables, roles and responsibilities been clearly communicated to every participant?

587. Who is involved?

588. What areas would you highlight for changes or improvements?

589. Does your vision/mission support a culture of quality data?

590. Be specific; avoid generalities. Thank you and great work alone are insufficient. What exactly do you appreciate and why?

591. Are the quality assurance functions and related roles and responsibilities clearly defined?

592. What should you highlight for improvement?

# 2.29 Human Resource Management Plan: knowledge assets

593. Is the manpower level sufficient to meet the future business requirements?

594. Has your organization readiness assessment been conducted?

595. Is the steering committee active in knowledge assets project oversight?

596. Is there a formal set of procedures supporting Stakeholder Management?

597. Has the budget been baselined?

598. What talent is needed?

599. Where is your organization headed?

600. Is there a set of procedures to capture, analyze and act on quality metrics?

601. Does the knowledge assets project have a formal knowledge assets project Charter?

602. Is quality monitored from the perspective of the customers needs and expectations?

603. Are changes in deliverable commitments agreed to by all affected groups & individuals?

604. Is knowledge assets project status reviewed with the steering and executive teams at appropriate intervals?

605. List roles. what commitments have been made?

606. knowledge assets project Objectives?

607. Who needs training?

608. Have knowledge assets project team accountabilities & responsibilities been clearly defined?

609. How relevant is this attribute to this knowledge assets project or audit?

# 2.30 Communications Management Plan: knowledge assets

610. Why manage stakeholders?

611. Do you feel a register helps?

612. Which stakeholders can influence others?

613. Who to learn from?

614. Are others needed?

615. What to know?

616. Who did you turn to if you had questions?

617. Are the stakeholders getting the information others need, are others consulted, are concerns addressed?

618. Can you think of other people who might have concerns or interests?

619. What help do you and your team need from the stakeholder?

620. Why do you manage communications?

621. Are there too many who have an interest in some aspect of your work?

622. Who is the stakeholder?

623. Why is stakeholder engagement important?

624. What are the interrelationships?

625. Do you have members of your team responsible for certain stakeholders?

626. How were corresponding initiatives successful?

627. Are others part of the communications management plan?

628. What is the political influence?

## 2.31 Risk Management Plan: knowledge assets

629. Was an original risk assessment/risk management plan completed?

630. Do you have a mechanism for managing change?

631. Why do you want risk management?

632. Are the metrics meaningful and useful?

633. For software; are compilers and code generators available and suitable for the product to be built?

634. Management -what contingency plans do you have if the risk becomes a reality?

635. Premium on reliability of product?

636. Market risk: will the new product be useful to your organization or marketable to others?

637. Why do you need to manage knowledge assets project Risk?

638. How is risk identification performed?

639. Does the knowledge assets project have the authority and ability to avoid the risk?

640. Is the customer willing to commit significant time to the requirements gathering process?

641. How is risk monitoring performed?

642. Market risk -will the new service or product be useful to your organization or marketable to others?

643. Are you on schedule?

644. Who should be notified of the occurrence of each of the indicators?

645. What risks are necessary to achieve success?

646. What would you do?

647. Where do risks appear in the business phases?

# 2.32 Risk Register: knowledge assets

648. What has changed since the last period?

649. Technology risk -is the knowledge assets project technically feasible?

650. Budget and schedule: what are the estimated costs and schedules for performing risk-related activities?

651. What could prevent you delivering on the strategic program objectives and what is being done to mitigate corresponding issues?

652. How well are risks controlled?

653. Are there other alternative controls that could be implemented?

654. What action, if any, has been taken to respond to the risk?

655. Methodology: how will risk management be performed on this knowledge assets project?

656. Assume the event happens, what is the Most Likely impact?

657. Who needs to know about this?

658. People risk -are people with appropriate skills available to help complete the knowledge assets project?

659. What evidence do you have to justify the likelihood score of the risk (audit, incident report, claim, complaints, inspection, internal review)?

660. What is a Community Risk Register?

661. Are implemented controls working as others should?

662. Financial risk -can your organization afford to undertake the knowledge assets project?

663. Schedule impact/severity estimated range (workdays) assume the event happens, what is the potential impact?

664. Severity Prediction?

665. Can the likelihood and impact of failing to achieve corresponding recommendations and action plans be assessed?

666. Are your objectives at risk?

667. Contingency actions - planned actions to reduce the immediate seriousness of the risk when it does occur. What should you do when?

# 2.33 Probability and Impact Assessment: knowledge assets

668. Are enough people available?

669. Is the customer willing to establish rapid communication links with the developer?

670. My knowledge assets project leader has suddenly left your organization, what do you do?

671. Are there alternative opinions/solutions/ processes you should explore?

672. How solid is the knowledge assets projection of competitive reaction?

673. What risks does your organization have if the knowledge assets projects fail to meet deadline?

674. Can you stabilize dynamic risk factors?

675. How will economic events and trends likely affect the knowledge assets project?

676. Are tool mentors available?

677. Is it necessary to deeply assess all knowledge assets project risks?

678. What is the likely future demand of the customer?

679. Do benefits and chances of success outweigh potential damage if success is not attained?

680. Prioritized components/features?

681. How do risks change during the knowledge assets projects life cycle?

682. What risks does the employee encounter?

683. Have decisions that should be left open because of inadequate information on technology been identified and responsibility assigned for reducing the uncertainty?

684. What would be the effect of slippage?

685. How well is the risk understood?

686. Does the software interface with new or unproven hardware or unproven vendor products?

687. Is the process supported by tools?

## 2.34 Probability and Impact Matrix: knowledge assets

688. What will be cost of redeployment of the personnel?

689. What can you use the analyzed risks for?

690. What is the political situation at present?

691. How do you manage knowledge assets project Risk?

692. What is the risk appetite?

693. What should you do FIRST?

694. To what extent is the chosen technology maturing?

695. How solid is the knowledge assets projection of competitive reaction?

696. How is the knowledge assets project going to be managed?

697. What action would you take to the identified risks in the knowledge assets project?

698. During knowledge assets project executing, a team member identifies a risk that is not in the risk register. What should you do?

699. Mandated delivery date?

700. Is the customer technically sophisticated in the product area?

701. What do you expect?

702. Are there new risks that mitigation strategies might introduce?

703. What are the risks involved in appointing external agencies to manage the knowledge assets project?

704. What are the levels of understanding of the future users of this technology?

705. Is the delay in one subknowledge assets project going to affect another?

# 2.35 Risk Data Sheet: knowledge assets

706. Who has a vested interest in how you perform as your organization (our stakeholders)?

707. What are you trying to achieve (Objectives)?

708. What if client refuses?

709. What are you weak at and therefore need to do better?

710. What is the chance that it will happen?

711. What do you know?

712. What are the main threats to your existence?

713. Whom do you serve (customers)?

714. Do effective diagnostic tests exist?

715. Risk of what?

716. How do you handle product safely?

717. What are your core values?

718. What can you do?

719. How reliable is the data source?

720. Potential for recurrence?

721. What will be the consequences if the risk happens?

722. What do people affected think about the need for, and practicality of preventive measures?

723. Will revised controls lead to tolerable risk levels?

724. What are the main opportunities available to you that you should grab while you can?

725. Type of risk identified?

## 2.36 Procurement Management Plan: knowledge assets

726. Is it possible to track all classes of knowledge assets project work (e.g. scheduled, un-scheduled, defect repair, etc.)?

727. Does the knowledge assets project have a formal knowledge assets project Charter?

728. Are meeting minutes captured and sent out after meetings?

729. Are the budget estimates reasonable?

730. Is the quality assurance team identified?

731. Are knowledge assets project contact logs kept up to date?

732. Are non-critical path items updated and agreed upon with the teams?

733. What areas are overlooked on this knowledge assets project?

734. Is the structure for tracking the knowledge assets project schedule well defined and assigned to a specific individual?

735. Is a payment system in place with proper reviews and approvals?

736. Does the resource management plan include a personnel development plan?

737. Does the knowledge assets project team have the right skills?

738. Are quality inspections and review activities listed in the knowledge assets project schedule(s)?

739. Have all involved knowledge assets project stakeholders and work groups committed to the knowledge assets project?

740. Are stakeholders aware and supportive of the principles and practices of modern software estimation?

## 2.37 Source Selection Criteria: knowledge assets

741. Do you want to wait until all offerors have been evaluated?

742. What common questions or problems are associated with debriefings?

743. What management structure does your organization consider as optimal for performing the contract?

744. What should be considered when developing evaluation standards?

745. What instructions should be provided regarding oral presentations?

746. What are the special considerations for preaward debriefings?

747. How should the solicitation aspects regarding past performance be structured?

748. What information may not be provided?

749. What documentation is necessary regarding electronic communications?

750. When must you conduct a debriefing?

751. How do you manage procurement?

752. Do you ensure you evaluate what you asked for, not what you want to see or expect to see?

753. Can you reasonably estimate total organization requirements for the coming year?

754. How can the methods of publicizing the buy be tailored to yield more effective price competition?

755. How are clarifications and communications appropriately used?

756. How should the oral presentations be handled?

757. What is the last item a knowledge assets project manager must do to finalize knowledge assets project close-out?

758. What are the limitations on pre-competitive range communications?

759. Are they compliant with all technical requirements?

760. What documentation is needed for a tradeoff decision?

## 2.38 Stakeholder Management Plan: knowledge assets

761. Are decisions captured in a decisions log?

762. Are parking lot items captured?

763. Are risk triggers captured?

764. Are the knowledge assets project plans updated on a frequent basis?

765. What is the general purpose in defining responsibilities of the already stated affiliated with the knowledge assets project?

766. Are all resource assumptions documented?

767. Who is gathering information?

768. Has a knowledge assets project Communications Plan been developed?

769. Have knowledge assets project success criteria been defined?

770. Are knowledge assets project contact logs kept up to date?

771. Is there an on-going process in place to monitor knowledge assets project risks?

772. Does this include subcontracted development?

773. Is a pmo (knowledge assets project management office) in place and does it provide oversight to the knowledge assets project?

774. How is information analyzed, and what specific pieces of data would be of interest to the knowledge assets project manager?

## 2.39 Change Management Plan: knowledge assets

775. Who should be involved in developing a change management strategy?

776. What would be an estimate of the total cost for the activities required to carry out the change initiative?

777. What are the training strategies?

778. When developing your communication plan do you address : When should the given message be communicated?

779. What new behaviours are required?

780. What is the most cynical response it can receive?

781. What new competencies will be required for the roles?

782. Has a training need analysis been carried out?

783. What is the worst thing that can happen if you communicate information?

784. What type of materials/channels will be available to leverage?

785. Is a training information sheet available?

786. Are work location changes required?

787. What are the major changes to processes?

788. When does it make sense to customize?

789. Has an information & communications plan been developed?

790. When should a given message be communicated?

791. What are the specific target groups/audiences that will be impacted by this change?

792. Who will do the training?

# 3.0 Executing Process Group: knowledge assets

793. What are the typical knowledge assets project management skills?

794. Specific - is the objective clear in terms of what, how, when, and where the situation will be changed?

795. Why do you need a good WBS to use knowledge assets project management software?

796. What will you do to minimize the impact should a risk event occur?

797. Have operating capacities been created and/or reinforced in partners?

798. Do the partners have sufficient financial capacity to keep up the benefits produced by the programme?

799. Does the case present a realistic scenario?

800. Is the knowledge assets project making progress in helping to achieve the set results?

801. How well defined and documented were the knowledge assets project management processes you chose to use?

802. What are the challenges knowledge assets project teams face?

803. What does it mean to take a systems view of a knowledge assets project?

804. Do your results resemble a normal distribution?

805. How could you control progress of your knowledge assets project?

806. Will a new application be developed using existing hardware, software, and networks?

807. Who will provide training?

808. Could a new application negatively affect the current IT infrastructure?

809. How do you prevent staff are just doing busywork to pass the time?

810. What are the main types of goods and services being outsourced?

811. What are crucial elements of successful knowledge assets project plan execution?

812. Based on your knowledge assets project communication management plan, what worked well?

# 3.1 Team Member Status Report: knowledge assets

813. Do you have an Enterprise knowledge assets project Management Office (EPMO)?

814. How it is to be done?

815. Is there evidence that staff is taking a more professional approach toward management of your organizations knowledge assets projects?

816. Are the attitudes of staff regarding knowledge assets project work improving?

817. When a teams productivity and success depend on collaboration and the efficient flow of information, what generally fails them?

818. What specific interest groups do you have in place?

819. Does every department have to have a knowledge assets project Manager on staff?

820. Why is it to be done?

821. Will the staff do training or is that done by a third party?

822. Does the product, good, or service already exist within your organization?

823. How can you make it practical?

824. How will resource planning be done?

825. The problem with Reward & Recognition Programs is that the truly deserving people all too often get left out. How can you make it practical?

826. What is to be done?

827. Are your organizations knowledge assets projects more successful over time?

828. How does this product, good, or service meet the needs of the knowledge assets project and your organization as a whole?

829. Does your organization have the means (staff, money, contract, etc.) to produce or to acquire the product, good, or service?

830. How much risk is involved?

831. Are the products of your organizations knowledge assets projects meeting customers objectives?

## 3.2 Change Request: knowledge assets

832. What are the Impacts to your organization?

833. Will all change requests and current status be logged?

834. Who can suggest changes?

835. What should be regulated in a change control operating instruction?

836. How fast will change requests be approved?

837. Has the change been highlighted and documented in the CSCI?

838. Should a more thorough impact analysis be conducted?

839. Will new change requests be acknowledged in a timely manner?

840. Are you implementing itil processes?

841. How can changes be graded?

842. Since there are no change requests in your knowledge assets project at this point, what must you have before you begin?

843. Who is included in the change control team?

844. How does a team identify the discrete elements of a configuration?

845. What is the relationship between requirements attributes and attributes like complexity and size?

846. Should staff call into the helpdesk or go to the website?

847. Will this change conflict with other requirements changes (e.g., lead to conflicting operational scenarios)?

848. How does your organization control changes before and after software is released to a customer?

849. What mechanism is used to appraise others of changes that are made?

850. Does the schedule include knowledge assets project management time and change request analysis time?

# 3.3 Change Log: knowledge assets

851. How does this relate to the standards developed for specific business processes?

852. Is the change request open, closed or pending?

853. How does this change affect the timeline of the schedule?

854. When was the request approved?

855. Is the change backward compatible without limitations?

856. Does the suggested change request seem to represent a necessary enhancement to the product?

857. Is this a mandatory replacement?

858. Is the change request within knowledge assets project scope?

859. Is the submitted change a new change or a modification of a previously approved change?

860. Do the described changes impact on the integrity or security of the system?

861. Does the suggested change request represent a desired enhancement to the products functionality?

862. Will the knowledge assets project fail if the change request is not executed?

863. Who initiated the change request?

864. When was the request submitted?

865. Where do changes come from?

866. Is the requested change request a result of changes in other knowledge assets project(s)?

867. How does this change affect scope?

# 3.4 Decision Log: knowledge assets

868. At what point in time does loss become unacceptable?

869. Linked to original objective?

870. How consolidated and comprehensive a story can you tell by capturing currently available incident data in a central location and through a log of key decisions during an incident?

871. Who is the decisionmaker?

872. How does the use a Decision Support System influence the strategies/tactics or costs?

873. How does an increasing emphasis on cost containment influence the strategies and tactics used?

874. Does anything need to be adjusted?

875. With whom was the decision shared or considered?

876. Decision-making process; how will the team make decisions?

877. It becomes critical to track and periodically revisit both operational effectiveness; Are you noticing all that you need to, and are you interpreting what you see effectively?

878. What is the line where eDiscovery ends and document review begins?

879. Who will be given a copy of this document and where will it be kept?

880. How does provision of information, both in terms of content and presentation, influence acceptance of alternative strategies?

881. Behaviors; what are guidelines that the team has identified that will assist them with getting the most out of team meetings?

882. How do you define success?

883. What alternatives/risks were considered?

884. Which variables make a critical difference?

885. What are the cost implications?

886. How effective is maintaining the log at facilitating organizational learning?

887. Adversarial environment. is your opponent open to a non-traditional workflow, or will it likely challenge anything you do?

# 3.5 Quality Audit: knowledge assets

888. How does your organization know that its Governance system is appropriately effective and constructive?

889. How does your organization know that its Strategic Plan is providing the best guidance for the future of your organization?

890. How does your organization know that its relationships with relevant professional bodies are appropriately effective and constructive?

891. How does your organization know that its security arrangements are appropriately effective and constructive?

892. How does your organization know that the range and quality of its social and recreational services and facilities are appropriately effective and constructive in meeting the needs of staff?

893. What experience do staff have in the type of work that the audit entails?

894. Does the supplier use a formal quality system?

895. What does the organizarion look for in a Quality audit?

896. Have personnel cleanliness and health requirements been established?

897. How does your organization know that its general support services planning and management systems are appropriately effective and constructive?

898. What mechanisms exist for identification of staff development needs?

899. What are you trying to do?

900. Are people allowed to contribute ideas?

901. Is the reports overall tone appropriate?

902. Are measuring and test equipment that have been placed out of service suitably identified and excluded from use in any device reconditioning operation?

903. How does your organization know that its system for managing intellectual property issues is appropriately effective, constructive and fair?

904. What data about organizational performance is routinely collected and reported?

905. How are you auditing your organizations compliance with regulations?

906. Are storage areas and reconditioning operations designed to prevent mix-ups and assure orderly handling of both the distressed and reconditioned devices?

907. How does your organization know that its staff support services planning and management systems are appropriately effective and constructive?

# 3.6 Team Directory: knowledge assets

908. Do purchase specifications and configurations match requirements?

909. When will you produce deliverables?

910. Process decisions: are there any statutory or regulatory issues relevant to the timely execution of work?

911. Timing: when do the effects of communication take place?

912. Who will write the meeting minutes and distribute?

913. What are you going to deliver or accomplish?

914. Decisions: is the most suitable form of contract being used?

915. How do unidentified risks impact the outcome of the knowledge assets project?

916. Does a knowledge assets project team directory list all resources assigned to the knowledge assets project?

917. Process decisions: is work progressing on schedule and per contract requirements?

918. Have you decided when to celebrate the knowledge assets projects completion date?

919. When does information need to be distributed?

920. Where should the information be distributed?

921. How and in what format should information be presented?

922. Who is the Sponsor?

923. Who should receive information (all stakeholders)?

924. Process decisions: which organizational elements and which individuals will be assigned management functions?

925. Who will be the stakeholders on your next knowledge assets project?

926. Process decisions: are all start-up, turn over and close out requirements of the contract satisfied?

# 3.7 Team Operating Agreement: knowledge assets

927. What is the anticipated procedure (recruitment, solicitation of volunteers, or assignment) for selecting team members?

928. What are some potential sources of conflict among team members?

929. Does your team need access to all documents and information at all times?

930. Did you draft the meeting agenda?

931. Do you prevent individuals from dominating the meeting?

932. Do you record meetings for the already stated unable to attend?

933. Do you leverage technology engagement tools group chat, polls, screen sharing, etc.?

934. Do you post any action items, due dates, and responsibilities on the team website?

935. Do team members reside in more than two countries?

936. Do you listen for voice tone and word choice to understand the meaning behind words?

937. How will group handle unplanned absences?

938. Do you upload presentation materials in advance and test the technology?

939. Do you begin with a question to engage everyone?

940. Did you recap the meeting purpose, time, and expectations?

941. What individual strengths does each team member bring to the group?

942. Communication protocols: how will the team communicate?

943. Are there more than two native languages represented by your team?

944. What administrative supports will be put in place to support the team and the teams supervisor?

945. Reimbursements: how will the team members be reimbursed for expenses and time commitments?

# 3.8 Team Performance Assessment: knowledge assets

946. To what degree does the teams work approach provide opportunity for members to engage in fact-based problem solving?

947. Lack of method variance in self-reported affect and perceptions at work: Reality or artifact?

948. To what degree can team members meet frequently enough to accomplish the teams ends?

949. If you are worried about method variance before you collect data, what sort of design elements might you include to reduce or eliminate the threat of method variance?

950. To what degree does the teams work approach provide opportunity for members to engage in results-based evaluation?

951. How do you recognize and praise members for contributions?

952. Social categorization and intergroup behaviour: Does minimal intergroup discrimination make social identity more positive?

953. What do you think is the most constructive thing that could be done now to resolve considerations and disputes about method variance?

954. If you have criticized someones work for method variance in your role as reviewer, what was the circumstance?

955. Is there a particular method of data analysis that you would recommend as a means of demonstrating that method variance is not of great concern for a given dataset?

956. To what degree does the teams approach to its work allow for modification and improvement over time?

957. To what degree are staff involved as partners in the improvement process?

958. To what degree does the teams purpose constitute a broader, deeper aspiration than just accomplishing short-term goals?

959. Do you promptly inform members about major developments that may affect them?

960. How does knowledge assets project termination impact knowledge assets project team members?

961. To what degree are sub-teams possible or necessary?

962. How much interpersonal friction is there in your team?

963. If you have received criticism from reviewers that your work suffered from method variance, what was the circumstance?

964. To what degree do team members agree with the goals, relative importance, and the ways in which achievement will be measured?

965. How do you keep key people outside the group informed about its accomplishments?

# 3.9 Team Member Performance Assessment: knowledge assets

966. How should adaptive assessments be implemented?

967. What innovations (if any) are developed to realize goals?

968. To what extent are systems and applications (e.g., game engine, mobile device platform) utilized?

969. What is the large, desired outcome?

970. What is the target group for instruction (e.g., individual and collective or small team instruction)?

971. For what period of time is a member rated?

972. How do you work together to improve teaching and learning?

973. What tools are available to determine whether all contract functional and compliance areas of performance objectives, measures, and incentives have been met?

974. Verify business objectives. Are they appropriate, and well-articulated?

975. Does platform-specific assessment information contribute to training placement or tailoring of instruction (e.g. aptitude-treatment interaction)?

976. Does the rater (supervisor) have the authority or responsibility to tell an employee that the employees performance is unsatisfactory?

977. To what degree can team members frequently and easily communicate with one another?

978. What entity leads the process, selects a potential restructuring option and develops the plan?

979. What is the role of the Reviewer?

980. What are best practices in use for the performance measurement system?

981. How is the timing of assessments organized (e.g., pre/post-test, single point during training, multiple reassessment during training)?

982. How will you identify your Team Leaders?

983. What evaluation results did you have?

# 3.10 Issue Log: knowledge assets

984. Do you prepare stakeholder engagement plans?

985. How is this initiative related to other portfolios, programs, or knowledge assets projects?

986. What would have to change?

987. Why multiple evaluators?

988. How often do you engage with stakeholders?

989. How do you reply to this question; you am new here and managing this major program. How do you suggest you build your network?

990. Who is the issue assigned to?

991. Which stakeholders are thought leaders, influences, or early adopters?

992. What does the stakeholder need from the team?

993. Is there an important stakeholder who is actively opposed and will not receive messages?

994. Who have you worked with in past, similar initiatives?

995. What steps can you take for positive relationships?

996. How do you manage human resources?

997. Can an impact cause deviation beyond team, stage or knowledge assets project tolerances?

998. What are the stakeholders interrelationships?

999. Are they needed?

1000. Who is involved as you identify stakeholders?

# 4.0 Monitoring and Controlling Process Group: knowledge assets

1001. What factors are contributing to progress or delay in the achievement of products and results?

1002. What are the goals of the program?

1003. Did you implement the program as designed?

1004. Where is the Risk in the knowledge assets project?

1005. Measurable - are the targets measurable?

1006. How is agile program management done?

1007. Mitigate. what will you do to minimize the impact should a risk event occur?

1008. User: who wants the information and what are they interested in?

1009. What were things that you did well, and could improve, and how?

1010. What resources are necessary?

1011. What is the timeline for the knowledge assets project?

1012. Overall, how does the program function to serve the clients?

1013. How well did you do?

1014. What input will you be required to provide the knowledge assets project team?

1015. Based on your knowledge assets project communication management plan, what worked well?

1016. Change, where should you look for problems?

1017. How are you doing?

# 4.1 Project Performance Report: knowledge assets

1018. To what degree do members articulate the goals beyond the team membership?

1019. To what degree do team members articulate the teams work approach?

1020. To what degree are the skill areas critical to team performance present?

1021. To what degree are the structures of the formal organization consistent with the behaviors in the informal organization?

1022. To what degree do team members feel that the purpose of the team is important, if not exciting?

1023. To what degree does the information network communicate information relevant to the task?

1024. To what degree do team members understand one anothers roles and skills?

1025. To what degree does the formal organization make use of individual resources and meet individual needs?

1026. To what degree does the teams work approach provide opportunity for members to engage in open interaction?

1027. To what degree do team members frequently explore the teams purpose and its implications?

1028. To what degree is the team cognizant of small wins to be celebrated along the way?

1029. To what degree will the team adopt a concrete, clearly understood, and agreed-upon approach that will result in achievement of the teams goals?

1030. To what degree do the structures of the formal organization motivate taskrelevant behavior and facilitate task completion?

1031. To what degree will the approach capitalize on and enhance the skills of all team members in a manner that takes into consideration other demands on members of the team?

1032. What is the PRS?

1033. To what degree does the task meet individual needs?

# 4.2 Variance Analysis: knowledge assets

1034. What can be the cause of an increase in costs?

1035. Contract line items and end items?

1036. What is exceptional?

1037. Are your organizations and items of cost assigned to each pool identified?

1038. Are there externalities from having some customers, even if they are unprofitable in the short run?

1039. Why do variances exist?

1040. Wbs elements contractually specified for reporting of status to your organization (lowest level only)?

1041. Budget versus actual. how does the monthly budget compare to actual experience?

1042. Is work progressively subdivided into detailed work packages as requirements are defined?

1043. Other relevant issues of Variance Analysis -selling price or gross margin?

1044. Are there changes in the overhead pool and/or organization structures?

1045. Can process improvements lead to unfavorable variances?

1046. Are the actual costs used for variance analysis reconcilable with data from the accounting system?

1047. What costs are avoidable if one or more customers are dropped?

1048. Are all authorized tasks assigned to identified organizational elements?

1049. How do you identify and isolate causes of favorable and unfavorable cost and schedule variances?

1050. Is cost and schedule performance measurement done in a consistent, systematic manner?

1051. Are all elements of indirect expense identified to overhead cost budgets of knowledge assets projections?

1052. Are the requirements for all items of overhead established by rational, traceable processes?

# 4.3 Earned Value Status: knowledge assets

1053. What is the unit of forecast value?

1054. How does this compare with other knowledge assets projects?

1055. Are you hitting your knowledge assets projects targets?

1056. Validation is a process of ensuring that the developed system will actually achieve the stakeholders desired outcomes; Are you building the right product? What do you validate?

1057. If earned value management (EVM) is so good in determining the true status of a knowledge assets project and knowledge assets project its completion, why is it that hardly any one uses it in information systems related knowledge assets projects?

1058. Earned value can be used in almost any knowledge assets project situation and in almost any knowledge assets project environment. it may be used on large knowledge assets projects, medium sized knowledge assets projects, tiny knowledge assets projects (in cut-down form), complex and simple knowledge assets projects and in any market sector. some people, of course, know all about earned value, they have used it for years - but perhaps not as effectively as they could have?

1059. Where is evidence-based earned value in your organization reported?

1060. Verification is a process of ensuring that the developed system satisfies the stakeholders agreements and specifications; Are you building the product right? What do you verify?

1061. When is it going to finish?

1062. Where are your problem areas?

1063. How much is it going to cost by the finish?

# 4.4 Risk Audit: knowledge assets

1064. Are requirements fully understood by the team and customers?

1065. Are regular safety inspections made of buildings, grounds and equipment?

1066. Does the implementation method matter?

1067. Are all financial transactions accurately recorded (receipted, banked)?

1068. Does willful intent modify risk-based auditing?

1069. What does monitoring consist of?

1070. Is all expenditure authorised through an identified process?

1071. What are risks and how do you manage them?

1072. Are your rules, by-laws and practices non-discriminatory?

1073. Do you have an understanding of insurance claims processes?

1074. Does the customer have a solid idea of what is required?

1075. If applicable; are compilers and code generators available and suitable for the product to be built?

1076. To what extent should analytical procedures be utilized in the risk-assessment process?

1077. Do you manage the process through use of metrics?

1078. Do you conduct risk assessments on all programs, activities and events?

1079. Do requirements demand the use of new analysis, design, or testing methods?

1080. Are all programs planned and conducted according to recognized safety standards?

1081. How do you compare to other jurisdictions when managing the risk of ....?

1082. Estimated size of product in number of programs, files, transactions?

1083. Do your financial policies and procedures ensure that each step in financial handling (receipt, recording, banking, reporting) is not completed by one person?

# 4.5 Contractor Status Report: knowledge assets

1084. What process manages the contracts?

1085. What was the final actual cost?

1086. Describe how often regular updates are made to the proposed solution. Are corresponding regular updates included in the standard maintenance plan?

1087. If applicable; describe your standard schedule for new software version releases. Are new software version releases included in the standard maintenance plan?

1088. How is risk transferred?

1089. How long have you been using the services?

1090. What was the actual budget or estimated cost for your organizations services?

1091. What are the minimum and optimal bandwidth requirements for the proposed solution?

1092. Are there contractual transfer concerns?

1093. What was the budget or estimated cost for your organizations services?

1094. Who can list a knowledge assets project as organization experience, your organization or a previous employee of your organization?

1095. What was the overall budget or estimated cost?

1096. What is the average response time for answering a support call?

# 4.6 Formal Acceptance: knowledge assets

1097. Do you buy pre-configured systems or build your own configuration?

1098. How well did the team follow the methodology?

1099. Was business value realized?

1100. What can you do better next time?

1101. What are the requirements against which to test, Who will execute?

1102. What lessons were learned about your knowledge assets project management methodology?

1103. Did the knowledge assets project achieve its MOV?

1104. What features, practices, and processes proved to be strengths or weaknesses?

1105. Who supplies data?

1106. Does it do what knowledge assets project team said it would?

1107. What is the Acceptance Management Process?

1108. Was the client satisfied with the knowledge

assets project results?

1109. Was the knowledge assets project managed well?

1110. Was the sponsor/customer satisfied?

1111. Have all comments been addressed?

1112. Did the knowledge assets project manager and team act in a professional and ethical manner?

1113. What function(s) does it fill or meet?

1114. Do you perform formal acceptance or burn-in tests?

1115. Is formal acceptance of the knowledge assets project product documented and distributed?

1116. Do you buy-in installation services?

# 5.0 Closing Process Group: knowledge assets

1117. Will the knowledge assets project deliverable(s) replace a current asset or group of assets?

1118. What could have been improved?

1119. What is the risk of failure to your organization?

1120. Did the knowledge assets project management methodology work?

1121. Were sponsors and decision makers available when needed outside regularly scheduled meetings?

1122. Were the outcomes different from the already stated planned?

1123. What could be done to improve the process?

1124. Was the schedule met?

1125. If action is called for, what form should it take?

1126. What were the desired outcomes?

1127. Is this a follow-on to a previous knowledge assets project?

1128. If a risk event occurs, what will you do?

1129. What is the knowledge assets project

Management Process?

1130. What can you do better next time, and what specific actions can you take to improve?

1131. Did the knowledge assets project team have the right skills?

1132. Can the lesson learned be replicated?

1133. Does the close educate others to improve performance?

# 5.1 Procurement Audit: knowledge assets

1134. Was the decision on the award process accurate and adequately communicated?

1135. Where required, were candidates registered as approved contractors, suppliers or service providers or certified by relevant bodies?

1136. Are periodic audits made of disbursement activities?

1137. Is it calculated whether aggregated procurement can be more cost-efficient?

1138. Has it been determined how large a portion of the procurement portfolio should be managed by the procurement function/unit and how large a portion that should be managed locally?

1139. Do staff involved in the various stages of the process have the appropriate skills and training to perform duties effectively?

1140. Audits: when was your last independent public accountant (ipa) audit and what were the results?

1141. Did your organization calculate the contract value accurately?

1142. Are the financial and business records of your organization stored in a secure fire resistant place?

1143. Were calculations used in evaluation adequate and correct?

1144. Has the award included no items different from the already stated contained in bid specifications?

1145. Where applicable, did your organization adequately manage experts employed to assist in the procurement process?

1146. Did your organization decide for an appropriate and admissible procurement procedure?

1147. Are budget transfers within the general fund made for only the already stated items permitted by law and regulation?

1148. Is there an effective risk management system continuously monitoring procurement risk?

1149. Does the strategy ensure that needs are met, and not exceeded?

1150. Are the journals and ledgers kept current for all funds?

1151. Are there performance targets on value for money obtained and cost savings?

1152. Are all checks pre-numbered?

1153. Is there time waste during tendering?

## 5.2 Contract Close-Out: knowledge assets

1154. Parties: Authorized?

1155. How/when used ?

1156. How is the contracting office notified of the automatic contract close-out?

1157. Change in knowledge?

1158. Was the contract sufficiently clear so as not to result in numerous disputes and misunderstandings?

1159. Have all acceptance criteria been met prior to final payment to contractors?

1160. Are the signers the authorized officials?

1161. Parties: who is involved?

1162. Has each contract been audited to verify acceptance and delivery?

1163. Was the contract type appropriate?

1164. What happens to the recipient of services?

1165. Change in circumstances?

1166. Have all contracts been completed?

1167. Change in attitude or behavior?

1168. Was the contract complete without requiring numerous changes and revisions?

1169. How does it work?

1170. What is capture management?

1171. Have all contract records been included in the knowledge assets project archives?

1172. Have all contracts been closed?

1173. Why Outsource?

## 5.3 Project or Phase Close-Out: knowledge assets

1174. Were messages directly related to the release strategy or phases of the knowledge assets project?

1175. If you were the knowledge assets project sponsor, how would you determine which knowledge assets project team(s) and/or individuals deserve recognition?

1176. What are the mandatory communication needs for each stakeholder?

1177. What is the information level of detail required for each stakeholder?

1178. Complete yes or no?

1179. What hierarchical authority does the stakeholder have in your organization?

1180. What security considerations needed to be addressed during the procurement life cycle?

1181. How often did each stakeholder need an update?

1182. What was the preferred delivery mechanism?

1183. What is in it for you?

1184. What advantages do the an individual interview

have over a group meeting, and vice-versa?

1185. Which changes might a stakeholder be required to make as a result of the knowledge assets project?

1186. Did the knowledge assets project management methodology work?

1187. What are the informational communication needs for each stakeholder?

1188. What is a Risk Management Process?

1189. Is the lesson significant, valid, and applicable?

1190. Was the user/client satisfied with the end product?

1191. Who are the knowledge assets project stakeholders and what are roles and involvement?

1192. What was learned?

# 5.4 Lessons Learned: knowledge assets

1193. Does the lesson describe a function that would be done differently the next time?

1194. How well were expectations met regarding the frequency and content of information that was conveyed to by the knowledge assets project Manager?

1195. What were the most significant issues on this knowledge assets project?

1196. Where do you go from here?

1197. What is the distribution of authority?

1198. Overall, how effective were the efforts to prepare you and your organization for the impact of the product/service of the knowledge assets project?

1199. What were the challenges and pitfalls?

1200. What is the proportion of in-house and contractor personnel authorized for the knowledge assets project?

1201. How much communication is task-related?

1202. Were cost budgets met?

1203. How timely were Progress Reports provided

to the knowledge assets project Manager by Team Members?

1204. What rewards do the individuals seek?

1205. Was the necessary hardware, software, accommodation etc available?

1206. How timely was the training you received in preparation for the use of the product/service?

1207. How effective was the architecture/system design process?

1208. What things surprised you on the knowledge assets project that were not in the plan?

1209. How effective were Best Practices & Lessons Learned from prior knowledge assets projects utilized in this knowledge assets project?

1210. What mistakes did you successfully avoid making?

1211. What regulatory constraints impact the case?

1212. What is in the future?

# Index